VIVEK RA[

The Life and Times of an American Business Icon from Humble Roots to Greatness

Eduversity Press

Copyright

Table of Contents

*"The pursuit of excellence is the antidote to identity politics." - **Vivek Ramaswamy***

PROLOGUE

===

"The reasonable man adapts himself to the world; the unreasonable one persists in trying to adapt the world to himself. There, all progress depends on the unreasonable man." - **George Bernard Shaw**

===

Vivek Ramaswamy is an American entrepreneur and former Republican presidential candidate for 2024. He has Indian immigrant parents and graduated from Harvard and Yale Law School. Ramaswamy founded Roivant Sciences, a biotech company that developed FDA-approved drugs, and co-founded Strive, an asset management firm opposing "woke" investing trends. He's written books criticizing corporate social justice initiatives and identity politics. Ramaswamy advocates for free market principles and challenges environmental, social, and governance (ESG) initiatives in business and investing.

Vivek's early life was steeped in the values of hard work, education, and the pursuit of excellence. From a young age, he demonstrated an insatiable curiosity and a keen intellect that would later become hallmarks of his professional career. As a child of two cultures, Vivek developed a unique perspective that allowed him to see connections and opportunities where others saw only obstacles.

Vivek's academic prowess led him to Harvard University, where he distinguished himself not only in his studies but also in extracurricular activities. Here, he sowed the seeds of his future endeavors by grappling with questions about the intersection of business, science, and society. His subsequent time at Yale Law School further honed his analytical skills and deepened his understanding of the complex regulatory world that would later become a crucial arena for his innovative ideas.

But Vivek really took off in finance and pharmaceuticals. His tenure at a prominent hedge fund gave him invaluable insights into the workings of the healthcare industry, revealing both its potential and its limitations. This experience led to the founding of Roivant Sciences, a company that would revolutionize the approach to drug development.

Roivant's innovative model—acquiring and developing abandoned drug candidates—was met with initial skepticism. Yet, under Vivek's leadership, the company quickly proved its worth, breathing new life into potentially life-saving treatments that had been cast aside by larger pharmaceutical firms. This approach not only led to the development of crucial medications but also forced the entire industry to reassess its research and development strategies.

However, Vivek's influence extends far beyond the realm of pharmaceuticals. As his success grew, so did his voice in the broader conversation about the role of business in society. His outspoken criticism of what he termed "woke capitalism" and his advocacy for a more focused approach to corporate governance have sparked intense debates in boardrooms, business schools, and policy circles across the nation.

Through his book "Woke, Inc." and numerous public appearances, Vivek has challenged prevailing notions of corporate social responsibility. He argues passionately for a return to core business principles, asserting that companies can best serve society by excelling in their primary missions rather than trying to be all things to all people. These ideas have resonated with many, particularly young entrepreneurs seeking a new paradigm for business success.

Vivek's impact on the business world is perhaps best exemplified by the rise of what some call "Ramaswamy-style" startups—companies characterized by their laser focus on core competencies, emphasis on meritocracy, and commitment to creating genuine value. His ideas have not only influenced a new generation of entrepreneurs but have also begun to shape the curricula of leading business schools.

Yet, for all his success and influence, Vivek remains grounded in the values instilled in him by his parents. He is a vocal advocate for the American Dream, often speaking about the opportunities that allowed him, the son of immigrants, to rise to the pinnacle of American business. This personal narrative lends authenticity and power to his arguments about meritocracy and the need for a level playing field in business and society.

As Vivek's profile has grown, so too has his influence in the realm of public policy. His insights on issues ranging from drug pricing to patent reform have made him a sought-after voice in Washington, D.C. He has testified before Congress, advised policymakers, and contributed to the shaping of legislation that promises to have far-reaching effects on American innovation and competitiveness.

Throughout his meteoric rise, Vivek has remained a controversial figure. His ideas challenge deeply held beliefs about the role of corporations in addressing social issues, and his critiques of stakeholder capitalism have drawn both praise and criticism. Yet, even his detractors acknowledge the impact he has had on shaping the conversation about the future of American business.

As we step into the life and times of Vivek Ramaswamy, we enter on a journey that is as much about the transformation of American capitalism as it is about one man's remarkable ascent. From his humble beginnings in Ohio to his current status as a business icon and thought leader, Vivek's story offers invaluable insights into the changing world of American business and the enduring power of principled leadership.

This book offers an intimate look at the experiences, ideas, and decisions that have shaped Vivek Ramaswamy's career and philosophy. It explores the challenges he faced, the risks he took, and the values that guided him as he built Roivant Sciences and emerged as a leading voice in debates about corporate purpose and responsibility.

But more than just a recounting of past achievements, this book is an exploration of ideas that promise to shape the future of American business. Through Vivek's story, we gain a window into the forces driving innovation in the pharmaceutical industry, the evolving relationship between business and society, and the ongoing debate about the proper role of corporations in addressing social issues.

Whether you're an aspiring entrepreneur, a seasoned business leader, or simply someone interested in the forces shaping our economic world, Vivek Ramaswamy's journey offers valuable lessons and thought-provoking insights. His story is a reminder of the transformative power of ideas and the impact that one individual can have when they dare to challenge the status quo.

As you turn the pages of this book, prepare to be inspired, challenged, and enlightened. Vivek Ramaswamy's story is more than just a personal success; it's a chronicle of a changing America and a glimpse into the future of business in the 21st century.

CHAPTER 1

ROOTS AND HERITAGE

===

"The journey of a thousand miles begins with a single step." **- Lao Tzu**

===

Vivek Ramaswamy's roots trace back to a modest household in southern India, where his parents, Ganapathy and Geetha Ramaswamy, grew up. Ganapathy, a driven and ambitious young man, recognized early on that education was the key to unlocking a brighter future. He excelled in his studies, earning a degree in engineering from a prestigious Indian university. However, he knew that to truly reach his potential, he needed to broaden his horizons beyond the borders of his homeland.

In the late 1970s, Ganapathy made the life-altering decision to pursue further education in the United States. With little more than a suitcase full of dreams and a heart brimming with hope, he boarded a plane bound for Cincinnati, Ohio. The choice of destination was not random; Cincinnati was home to General Electric's aircraft engines division, a mecca for aspiring engineers from around the world.

Upon arrival, Ganapathy found himself in a world vastly different from the one he had left behind. The Midwestern world, with its sprawling suburbs and wide-open spaces, stood in stark contrast to the densely populated cities of India. Yet he was undeterred by the culture shock. Instead, he embraced the challenges with characteristic determination, throwing himself into his studies and working with unbridled enthusiasm.

While Ganapathy was laying the groundwork for his family's future in America, Geetha remained in India, pursuing her own dreams. She was a talented and ambitious woman in her own right; she had earned a degree in mathematics and had aspirations of becoming a computer programmer. The couple's separation was difficult, but they remained united by their shared vision of building a better life together.

After several years of hard work and perseverance, Ganapathy had established himself as a respected engineer at GE. It was then that he felt ready to bring Geetha with him to their new American home. Their reunion marked the beginning of a new chapter in the Ramaswamy family saga.

The couple settled into life in Cincinnati, a city that would become the backdrop for their American story. They embraced their new community while holding tight to their cultural heritage, creating a unique blend of Indian traditions and American values that would shape their future children's worldview.

It was into this rich cultural heritage that Vivek Ramaswamy was born in August 1985. From his earliest days, young Vivek was immersed in a world where the aroma of his mother's South Indian cooking mingled with the sounds of Midwestern twang floating through open windows. This dual heritage would become a defining feature of his identity, informing his perspectives and driving his ambitions in the years to come.

Growing up in Ohio, Vivek experienced a childhood that was both essentially American and distinctly Indian. His parents instilled in him a deep respect for education, hard work, and cultural values. Family dinners were often accompanied by lively discussions about politics, economics, and philosophy, nurturing Vivek's intellectual curiosity from a young age.

The Ramaswamy household was a hive of activity and learning. Geetha, having realized her dream of becoming a geriatric psychiatrist, balanced her demanding career with her role as a nurturing mother. She often brought home stories from her work, exposing Vivek to the complexities of the human mind and the importance of empathy in healthcare.

Ganapathy, meanwhile, continued to excel in his career at GE. His work ethic and innovative thinking set an example for his son, demonstrating the rewards of perseverance and outside-the-box thinking. He frequently brought Vivek to his workplace, allowing the young boy to marvel at the massive jet engines and sparking an early interest in science and technology.

Despite their professional success, the Ramaswamys never lost sight of their roots. They maintained close ties with their extended family in India, often hosting relatives for extended stays and organizing cultural events in their community. These experiences exposed Vivek to the richness of his heritage, instilling in him a sense of pride in his Indian background.

Vivek's childhood in Ohio was marked by a unique blend of experiences. He attended public schools, where he was often one of the few students of Indian descent. This position as a cultural bridge-builder helped shape his ability to navigate diverse environments, a skill that would serve him well in his future endeavors.

The young Ramaswamy showed early signs of the intellectual prowess and competitive spirit that would later define his career. He excelled in his studies, particularly in mathematics and science, often outpacing his peers. However, it wasn't just in academics that Vivek shone. He also developed a passion for tennis, spending countless hours on the court honing his skills. The discipline and strategic thinking required in tennis would later translate into his approach to business and life.

Ohio's heartland values of hard work, community, and perseverance deeply influenced Vivek's formative years. The state's rich history of innovation, from the Wright brothers to Neil Armstrong, served as a constant reminder of the potential for greatness that lay within reach of those willing to dream big and work hard.

Yet, growing up in Ohio also exposed Vivek to the challenges facing Middle America. He witnessed firsthand the impact of deindustrialization on local communities as factories closed and jobs disappeared. These experiences would later inform his views on economic policy and the role of business in society.

Vivek's intellectual curiosity led him to explore beyond the confines of his school curriculum. He became an avid reader, devouring books on a wide range of subjects, from classical literature to modern physics. His parents encouraged this thirst for knowledge, often engaging him in debates and discussions that challenged his thinking and honed his argumentative skills.

As Vivek entered his teenage years, he began to display the entrepreneurial spirit that would later define his career. He started small businesses, from lawnmowing services to tutoring younger students, always looking for ways to create value and solve problems. These early ventures were more than just ways to earn pocket money; they were invaluable lessons in business fundamentals and customer service.

The Ramaswamy family's journey from India to Ohio is a testament to the power of the American dream. Through hard work, determination, and a willingness to embrace new challenges, Ganapathy and Geetha created a life for themselves and their children that spanned two cultures and opened doors to endless possibilities.

For Vivek, growing up in Ohio as the child of immigrants provided a unique perspective on American life. He learned to appreciate the opportunities afforded by his adopted homeland while maintaining a deep connection to his Indian heritage. This dual identity would become a source of strength, allowing him to bridge cultural divides and see issues from multiple angles.

The values instilled in Vivek during his Ohio upbringing—hard work, innovation, and a sense of social responsibility—would form the foundation of his future success. The lessons learned at the dinner table, on the tennis court, and in the classrooms of Ohio would shape his approach to business, politics, and life.

As Vivek prepared to leave Ohio for college, he carried with him the dreams of his parents, the values of his Midwestern upbringing, and the rich cultural heritage of his Indian roots. This unique combination of influences would propel him onto the national stage, where he would make his mark as a business leader, author, and public intellectual.

The story of Vivek Ramaswamy is inextricably linked to the story of his family's journey and his Ohio upbringing. It's a narrative that embodies the best of the American experience—the idea that with hard work, determination, and a bit of luck, anyone can rise from humble beginnings to achieve greatness.

From Vivek's roots and heritage, we've seen how the seeds of his future success were planted in the fertile soil of his family's immigrant experience and nurtured by the values of his Ohio upbringing. The journey that began with his parents' bold decision to seek a better life in America would continue through Vivek's own pursuit of excellence, guided by the lessons learned in his formative years.

The story of the Ramaswamy family is more than just a tale of individual success; it's a testament to the enduring power of the American dream. It reminds us that our nation's strength lies in its ability to welcome newcomers and provide them with the opportunity to contribute their talents and perspectives to the grand experiment of American democracy.

As we follow Vivek's journey from these humble beginnings to the heights of American business and public life, we'll see how the values instilled in him during these early years in Ohio would shape his decisions, fuel his ambitions, and ultimately define his impact on the world. The roots planted in the heartland of America would grow into a legacy that spans industries, challenges conventional wisdom, and continues to inspire others to dream big and work hard in pursuit of their own American dream.

HIGHLIGHTS

1. Ganapathy Ramaswamy's bold decision to leave India for the United States in pursuit of better opportunities, settling in Cincinnati to work for General Electric's aircraft engines division.

2. The reunion of Ganapathy and Geetha in America and their efforts to blend Indian traditions with American values, creating a unique cultural environment for their children.

3. Vivek Ramaswamy's childhood in Ohio, marked by exposure to both Indian and American cultures, shaped his worldview and ability to navigate diverse environments.

4. The influence of Ohio's heartland values on Vivek, including hard work, community spirit, and perseverance, alongside exposure to the challenges facing Middle America.

QUESTIONS FOR READERS

1. How did the Ramaswamy family's immigrant experience shape Vivek's perspective on the American Dream?

   _____

   _____

   _____

   _____

   _____

2. What role did Ohio's cultural and economic world play in forming Vivek's values and ambitions?

   _____

   _____

   _____

   _____

   _____

3. How might Vivek's dual cultural heritage have influenced his approach to business and public life?

_____

_____

_____

_____

_____

4. What lessons can we draw from the Ramaswamy family's journey about the impact of parental influence and cultural background on a child's future success?

_____

_____

_____

_____

_____

CHAPTER 2

AN IGNITED MIND

==

"Education is not the filling of a pail, but the lighting of a fire." - **William Butler Yeats**

==

The story of Vivek's intellectual awakening begins in the classrooms of Cincinnati, Ohio. As a young student at William Mason High School, Vivek quickly distinguished himself as a prodigy with an insatiable curiosity. His teachers often remarked on his ability to grasp complex concepts with ease, whether in mathematics, science, or the humanities. But it wasn't just his academic prowess that set him apart; it was his unique way of approaching problems, always seeking to understand the underlying principles rather than simply memorizing facts.

One of Vivek's high school teachers, Mrs. Johnson, fondly remembers a moment that exemplified his exceptional mind. During a chemistry lesson on molecular structures, Vivek not only grasped the concept quickly but also proposed a novel way of visualizing complex molecules that helped his classmates understand the topic better. This ability to simplify complex ideas and share them with others would become a hallmark of his later career.

Outside the classroom, Vivek's parents played a crucial role in nurturing his intellectual growth. Dinner table conversations in the Ramaswamy household were far from ordinary. Ganapathy and Geetha Ramaswamy encouraged lively debates on topics ranging from politics and economics to philosophy and science. These discussions challenged young Vivek to think critically, articulate his thoughts clearly, and consider multiple perspectives—skills that would prove invaluable in his future endeavors.

Vivek's father, drawing from his engineering background, often presented his son with real-world problems to solve. One summer, he tasked Vivek with designing a more efficient sprinkler system for their backyard. This project not only honed Vivek's problem-solving skills but also introduced him to the principles of fluid dynamics and conservation—concepts that would later influence his approach to business efficiency.

His mother's influence was equally significant. She frequently shared stories from her work as a geriatric psychiatrist, exposing Vivek to the complexities of the human mind and the importance of empathy in healthcare. These early insights into the medical field would later play a crucial role in shaping Vivek's interest in the intersection of business and healthcare.

Vivek's intellectual pursuits weren't confined to the classroom or home. He became an avid participant in academic competitions, particularly excelling in debate and science fairs. In his sophomore year, he led his school's debate team to the state championships, showcasing his ability to construct compelling arguments and think on his feet. His performance caught the attention of local business leaders, one of whom offered Vivek a summer internship at a biotech startup.

This internship proved to be a pivotal moment in Vivek's life. For the first time, he was exposed to the exciting world of biotechnology and its potential to revolutionize healthcare. The experience opened his eyes to the possibility of combining his passion for science with his growing interest in business. He spent countless hours poring over scientific journals and business reports, eager to understand how scientific breakthroughs could be translated into viable commercial products.

Returning to school after the internship, Vivek approached his studies with renewed vigor. He convinced his school administration to allow him to take advanced placement courses in biology and economics simultaneously—an unusual combination that reflected his emerging interests. His economics teacher, Mr. Roberts, recalls Vivek's unique ability to draw parallels between biological systems and economic principles, often leading to fascinating class discussions.

It was during this time that Vivek also developed a keen interest in the stock market. He persuaded his parents to let him invest a small portion of his savings in stocks, but with a twist—he would only invest in biotech companies whose scientific papers he had read and understood. This self-imposed rule forced him to dive deep into the world of biotechnology, learning not just about the science but also about market dynamics, regulatory environments, and the challenges of bringing new drugs to market.

Vivek's extracurricular activities also reflected his growing passion for the intersection of science and business. He founded the school's first Biotech Club, which quickly became one of the most popular student organizations. Under his leadership, the club organized visits to local research laboratories, hosted guest lectures by industry professionals, and even initiated a small-scale research project studying the effects of local water quality on plant growth.

The club's crowning achievement came in Vivek's senior year when they organized a citywide Biotech Innovation Challenge. The event brought together students, researchers, and business leaders, showcasing the potential of biotechnology to solve real-world problems. Vivek's opening speech at the event, which eloquently articulated the promise of biotech innovation, caught the attention of a visiting professor from Harvard, who encouraged him to consider applying to the prestigious university.

As Vivek's high school years came to a close, his academic achievements were nothing short of stellar. He graduated as valedictorian, with perfect scores on both the SAT and ACT. But more importantly, he had discovered his true calling—a passion for leveraging scientific innovation to create meaningful change in the world.

Vivek's journey to Harvard marked the beginning of a new chapter in his life. The ivy-covered walls of the centuries-old institution offered an environment where his intellect could truly flourish. From the moment he set foot on campus, Vivek immersed himself in a diverse array of courses, from molecular biology to economic theory, always seeking to bridge the gap between scientific discovery and practical application.

It was at Harvard that Vivek's interdisciplinary approach to learning truly came into its own. He often surprised his professors by drawing unexpected connections between seemingly unrelated fields. In one memorable instance, he wrote a paper for his economics class that used principles of evolutionary biology to explain market behaviors during economic crises. The paper not only earned him top marks but also caught the attention of faculty members in both the economics and biology departments.

Vivek's time at Harvard was marked by an insatiable curiosity that extended far beyond the classroom. He became a fixture at guest lectures and seminars, often staying behind to engage speakers in deep discussions. One such encounter with a visiting biotech entrepreneur led to a summer internship at a cutting-edge gene therapy startup in Boston's booming biotech hub.

This internship provided Vivek with firsthand experience of the challenges and opportunities in bringing scientific innovations to market. He witnessed the complex interplay between scientific research, regulatory hurdles, and business strategies. The experience cemented his belief that there was a critical need for individuals who could bridge the gap between scientific innovation and business acumen.

Returning to Harvard for his final years, Vivek focused his studies on this intersection of science and business. He designed an interdisciplinary major that combined elements of biology, chemistry, economics, and business management. His thesis, which explored novel funding models for high-risk, high-reward biotech research, earned him the highest honors and was later published in a respected industry journal.

Throughout his time at Harvard, Vivek never lost sight of his roots or the values instilled in him by his parents. He remained actively involved in cultural organizations on campus, often serving as a bridge between different student groups. His ability to navigate diverse environments and bring people together would prove invaluable in his future career.

As graduation approached, Vivek faced a pivotal decision. He had offers from top investment banks and consulting firms, as well as acceptances to several prestigious graduate programs. However, inspired by his experiences and driven by a desire to make a tangible impact, he chose a different path. He decided to join a small biotech firm as a junior analyst, believing that this role would allow him to gain a comprehensive understanding of the industry from the ground up.

This decision raised eyebrows among some of his peers, who couldn't understand why someone with his credentials would choose a relatively low-profile position. But Vivek was playing the long game. He understood that to truly revolutionize an industry, one needed to understand its intricacies from every angle.

Vivek's early career was marked by the same intensity and curiosity that characterized his academic journey. He worked hard and was often the first and last to leave the office. His colleagues were impressed not just by his work ethic but also by his ability to quickly grasp complex scientific concepts and translate them into business strategies.

It was during this time that Vivek began to develop his unique approach to business and innovation. He observed that many promising scientific discoveries failed to reach the market due to a disconnect between researchers and business executives. He made it his mission to bridge this gap, often serving as a translator between the lab and the boardroom.

Vivek's innovative thinking and ability to spot untapped opportunities soon caught the attention of industry leaders. Within a few years, he had risen through the ranks, becoming one of the youngest executives in the biotech industry. His rapid ascent was fueled not just by his intellect but by his unwavering commitment to leveraging science for the betterment of society.

Looking back on his journey from a curious child in Ohio to a rising star in the biotech world, it's clear that Vivek's success was no accident. It was the result of a mindset ignited by a passion for learning, nurtured by supportive parents and mentors, and driven by a desire to make a meaningful impact on the world.

Vivek's story serves as an inspiration to aspiring entrepreneurs and innovators. It demonstrates the power of interdisciplinary thinking, the importance of hands-on experience, and the impact that one individual can have when they dare to challenge conventional wisdom.

The foundations laid during Vivek's formative years—his early education, his experiences at Harvard, and his first steps in the professional world—would prove crucial in his journey to becoming a business icon. They equipped him with the knowledge, skills, and perspective needed to navigate the complex world of modern business and drive meaningful change.

As we look ahead to Vivek's future accomplishments, we can see how these early experiences shaped the business leader he would become. His unique blend of scientific understanding and business acumen, his ability to bridge diverse fields, and his unwavering commitment to innovation would go on to redefine industries and challenge the status quo.

The story of Vivek Ramaswamy is far from over. But one thing is certain: the fire of curiosity and passion for knowledge ignited in his youth continues to burn bright, illuminating new paths and inspiring others to follow in his footsteps.

HIGHLIGHTS

1. Vivek's exceptional academic performance at William Mason High School, where he demonstrated a unique ability to grasp and simplify complex concepts, particularly in science and mathematics.

2. Vivek's parents' influential role in nurturing his intellectual growth through engaging dinner table discussions and real-world problem-solving challenges.

3. Vivek's pivotal internship at a biotech startup during high school sparked his passion for combining science with business and led to his self-directed study of biotechnology companies.

4. His founding of the Biotech Club at his high school and organization of the citywide Biotech Innovation Challenge showcased his early leadership skills and commitment to promoting scientific innovation.

QUESTIONS FOR READERS

1. How did Vivek's early exposure to diverse fields shape his unique approach to business and innovation?

   _____

   _____

   _____

   _____

   _____

2. What role did mentors and early experiences play in igniting Vivek's passion for biotechnology?

   _____

   _____

   _____

   _____

   _____

3. How might Vivek's decision to start at a junior position in a biotech firm, rather than accepting more prestigious offers, have influenced his career world?

_____

_____

_____

_____

_____

4. In what ways did Vivek's interdisciplinary approach to learning at Harvard prepare him for his future role as a business leader?

_____

_____

_____

_____

_____

CHAPTER 3

THE IVY LEAGUE YEARS

===

"Education is not preparation for life; education is life itself." - **John Dewey**

===

This profound statement by the American philosopher and educational reformer perfectly encapsulates Vivek Ramaswamy's approach to his Ivy League years. For Vivek, Harvard and Yale were not merely stepping stones to a successful career but transformative experiences that shaped his worldview, honed his intellect, and set the stage for his future as a business icon.

Vivek arrived at Harvard in the fall of 2003, his mind brimming with ideas and his heart full of ambition. The hallowed halls of this prestigious institution, which had nurtured countless leaders, innovators, and thinkers, now welcomed a young man from Ohio who was eager to make his mark on the world.

From the outset, Vivek's approach to his undergraduate studies was anything but conventional. While many of his peers chose to specialize early, Vivek embraced the liberal arts ethos of Harvard, diving into a diverse array of subjects with unbridled enthusiasm. He saw connections where others saw disparate fields, drawing insights from philosophy to inform his understanding of economics and applying principles of biology to his study of social systems.

One of Vivek's professors, Dr. Elizabeth Chen, recalls a particularly illuminating moment during a seminar on evolutionary biology. "Vivek raised his hand and drew a parallel between the adaptation of species and the evolution of market economies," she recounts. The perspective was new to us and led to one of the most engaging discussions we'd had all semester.

This interdisciplinary approach became Vivek's trademark. He was often seen hurrying across Harvard Yard, arms laden with books on subjects ranging from molecular biology to classical literature. His dorm room became a hub of intellectual discourse, where students from various departments would gather to debate ideas late into the night.

But Vivek's time at Harvard wasn't all academic pursuit. He threw himself into campus life with characteristic vigor, joining the debate team and quickly rising to prominence as one of its star members. His ability to construct compelling arguments and think on his feet, honed during his high school years, served him well in college competitions.

It was during a national debate tournament that Vivek first encountered the complex world of healthcare policy. The topic that year centered on reforming the U.S. healthcare system, and Vivek found himself fascinated by the intricate interplay of science, economics, and public policy. This experience would later prove instrumental in shaping his career path.

Outside of academics and debate, Vivek also discovered a passion for entrepreneurship. He co-founded a student organization called "Biotech Innovators," which brought together students interested in the intersection of biology and business. The group organized lectures by industry leaders, field trips to biotech startups, and even launched a small venture that aimed to develop affordable diagnostic tools for developing countries.

Vivek's summers were equally packed with formative experiences. After his sophomore year, he secured an internship at a leading hedge fund in New York. His exposure to the world of high finance opened his eyes to the power of capital markets in driving innovation and growth. However, it also left him with a nagging feeling that there had to be a more direct way to create value and impact lives.

The following summer, Vivek opted for a research position at a biotech firm in Cambridge. Here, he witnessed firsthand the challenges and triumphs of bringing cutting-edge scientific discoveries to market. This experience solidified his belief that his future lay at the intersection of science, business, and law.

As his time at Harvard drew to a close, Vivek found himself at a crossroads. He had offers from top consulting firms and investment banks, but a different path beckoned. The complexities of the healthcare system that he had encountered during his debate experiences, combined with his passion for biotechnology, led him to consider law school as the next step in his journey.

Yale Law School, with its reputation for fostering interdisciplinary thinking and its strong health law program, seemed like the perfect fit. Vivek's application essay, which argued for a new legal framework to accelerate biomedical innovation, caught the attention of the admissions committee. In the fall of 2007, Vivek found himself in New Haven, ready to embark on the next phase of his educational journey.

The transition from Harvard to Yale Law was not without its challenges. The rigor of legal education, with its emphasis on precise language and logical reasoning initially seemed at odds with Vivek's freewheeling, interdisciplinary approach. However, he soon came to appreciate how the discipline of legal thinking could sharpen his already formidable intellectual toolkit.

Professor Jonathan Marks, who taught Vivek in his first-year contracts class, remembers him as a student who constantly pushed the boundaries of legal reasoning. "Vivek had a knack for identifying the underlying principles behind legal rules and applying them in novel contexts," Marks recalls. "He wasn't content with merely learning the law; he wanted to understand its purpose and explore its potential for driving positive change."

Vivek's interest in healthcare and biotechnology found a natural home in Yale's Health Law program. He immersed himself in courses on FDA regulation, intellectual property law, and bioethics. His term paper on the legal and ethical implications of gene editing technology was later published in a leading law review, earning him recognition from both legal scholars and biotech industry leaders.

But Vivek's legal education wasn't confined to the classroom. He actively sought out practical experiences that would complement his academic studies. He spent one summer interning at the U.S. Patent and Trademark Office, gaining first-hand insight into the process of protecting intellectual property in the biotech industry. Another summer was devoted to working with a non-profit organization that provided legal aid to low-income patients navigating the healthcare system.

These experiences reinforced Vivek's belief in the power of law as a tool for social change. He began to envision a career that would allow him to leverage his unique combination of scientific knowledge, business acumen, and legal expertise to drive innovation in the healthcare sector.

Vivek's time at Yale also saw him develop as a leader and public speaker. He was elected president of the Yale Law School Student Association, a position that allowed him to advocate for student interests and organize events that brought together diverse perspectives on pressing legal and social issues.

One of the most memorable events of his tenure was a symposium on the future of healthcare innovation, which brought together leading figures from the worlds of medicine, law, and business. Vivek's opening address, which painted a bold vision of a healthcare system transformed by cutting-edge science and patient-centric policies, earned him a standing ovation and caught the attention of several industry leaders in attendance.

As graduation approached, Vivek found himself with a wealth of options. Top law firms were eager to recruit him, and several biotech companies had expressed interest in bringing him on board in a legal or business development capacity. However, true to form, Vivek was contemplating a less conventional path.

The idea that had been germinating since his Harvard days—of creating a new model for drug development that could bring life-saving treatments to market more quickly and efficiently—had grown into a full-fledged vision. Vivek believed that his unique background—spanning science, business, and now law—positioned him to tackle this challenge in a way that few others could.

In a move that surprised many of his classmates and professors, Vivek decided to forgo traditional career paths and instead pursue his vision of revolutionizing the biotech industry. He spent the months following graduation refining his ideas, networking with potential investors and partners, and laying the groundwork for what would become his first major venture.

Looking back on his Ivy League years, it's clear that Harvard and Yale played a crucial role in shaping Vivek Ramaswamy into the visionary leader he would become. These institutions provided not just knowledge and skills but also a platform for Vivek to explore, experiment, and refine his ideas.

At Harvard, Vivek learned the value of interdisciplinary thinking and developed his ability to draw insights from diverse fields. He honed his skills in debate and public speaking and discovered his passion for the intersection of science and business. The liberal arts education he received there gave him a broad perspective that would prove invaluable in his future endeavors.

Yale Law School, in turn, provided Vivek with the legal and analytical tools to navigate the complex regulatory world of the healthcare industry. It sharpened his ability to construct compelling arguments and identify innovative solutions to complex problems. Perhaps most importantly, it reinforced his belief in the power of law and policy to drive positive change in society.

Throughout his Ivy League journey, Vivek remained true to the values instilled in him by his parents: hard work, intellectual curiosity, and a commitment to making a positive impact on the world. He approached each new challenge with enthusiasm and determination, always seeking to push the boundaries of what was possible.

The connections Vivek made during these years—with professors, classmates, and industry leaders—would prove invaluable in his future career. Many of those who knew him during this time speak of his infectious enthusiasm, his ability to inspire others with his vision, and his unwavering commitment to his goals.

As Vivek stepped out of the Ivy League and into the world of business and entrepreneurship, he carried with him not just degrees from two of the world's most prestigious institutions but a wealth of experiences, ideas, and relationships that would serve as the foundation for his future success.

The young man from Ohio who had arrived at Harvard full of ambition and ideas had been transformed by his Ivy League years. He emerged as a leader with a unique vision, armed with the knowledge, skills, and networks to turn that vision into reality. The stage was set for Vivek Ramaswamy to make his mark on the world of business and beyond.

The impact of Vivek's Ivy League education would soon become evident as he embarked on his professional journey. The interdisciplinary approach he had cultivated at Harvard, combined with the sharp legal mind honed at Yale, provided him with a unique perspective on the challenges facing the healthcare and biotech industries.

Vivek's first major venture, launched shortly after his graduation from Yale Law School, was a bold attempt to reimagine the drug development process. Drawing on his understanding of science, business, and law, he proposed a new model that aimed to accelerate the pace of innovation while reducing costs. This venture, which initially raised eyebrows in the conservative pharmaceutical industry, would eventually grow into a multi-billion dollar enterprise.

But the true value of Vivek's Ivy League years extended far beyond the academic knowledge he had acquired. The networks he had built, the leadership skills he had developed, and the confidence he had gained in articulating and defending his ideas all played crucial roles in his rapid rise to prominence in the business world.

One of Vivek's Harvard classmates, now a successful venture capitalist, recalls a conversation they had during their senior year. "Vivek told me he wanted to change the world," she says. "At the time, I thought it was just youthful idealism. But looking at what he's accomplished, I realize he was dead serious—and he had the intellect and drive to make it happen."

Indeed, Vivek's Ivy League education had not only prepared him for success in the traditional sense but had also nurtured his desire to challenge the status quo and pursue bold, transformative ideas. The rigorous academic environment had taught him to think critically and approach problems from multiple angles, skills that would prove invaluable in his business career.

Moreover, the diverse experiences he had sought out during his time at Harvard and Yale—from debate competitions to entrepreneurial ventures to legal internships—had given him a breadth of perspective that set him apart from his peers. He was equally comfortable discussing the intricacies of molecular biology, the nuances of patent law, and the complexities of financial markets.

As Vivek's career progressed, he frequently drew upon the lessons learned during his Ivy League years. The ability to synthesize information from diverse sources, a skill he had honed in Harvard's liberal arts environment, allowed him to identify opportunities that others overlooked. The legal reasoning skills he developed at Yale enabled him to navigate complex regulatory worlds with confidence.

Vivek's Ivy League experience had instilled in him a sense of responsibility to use his talents and opportunities for the greater good. This ethos would become a defining feature of his business philosophy, driving him to pursue ventures that promised not just financial returns but also significant social impact.

The story of Vivek Ramaswamy's Ivy League years is more than just a tale of academic achievement. It's a testament to the transformative power of education when combined with ambition, curiosity, and a willingness to challenge conventional wisdom. From the lecture halls of Harvard to the moot courts of Yale, Vivek had not just gained knowledge—he had forged a vision for his future and developed the tools to bring that vision to life.

HIGHLIGHTS

1. Vivek's interdisciplinary approach at Harvard, where he connected diverse fields like biology, economics, and philosophy, setting him apart from his peers and foreshadowing his innovative thinking in business.

2. His co-founding of "Biotech Innovators" at Harvard demonstrated early leadership and entrepreneurial spirit in combining biology and business interests.

3. Vivek's experience at Yale Law School, where he applied his scientific and business knowledge to legal studies, particularly in health law and biotech regulation.

4. His summer internships, including positions at a hedge fund and a biotech firm, provided practical experience and shaped his future career path.

QUESTIONS FOR READERS

1. How did Vivek's interdisciplinary approach at Harvard contribute to his unique perspective in business and healthcare?

_____

_____

_____

_____

_____

2. In what ways did Vivek's experiences at Yale Law School complement his scientific and business background?

_____

_____

_____

_____

_____

3. How might Vivek's decision to pursue entrepreneurship over traditional career paths have influenced his future success?

_____

_____

_____

_____

_____

4. What role did extracurricular activities and internships play in shaping Vivek's vision and skills during his Ivy League years?

_____

_____

_____

_____

_____

CHAPTER 4

BEGINNINGS ON WALL STREET

==

"In the world of finance, the most valuable commodity is information." - **Michael Douglas as Gordon Gekko in "Wall Street"**

==

The gleaming glass towers of Wall Street loomed before Vivek Ramaswamy as he arrived in Lower Manhattan in the summer of 2007. Fresh from his Ivy League education, he was about to plunge into the high-stakes world of finance, a journey that would challenge his convictions and shape his future as a business icon.

Vivek's first stop on this financial pilgrimage was none other than Goldman Sachs, the venerable investment bank known for its cutthroat culture and unparalleled success. He had secured a coveted position in the bank's investment banking division, beating out thousands of other applicants for the opportunity to learn from the best in the business.

From day one, Vivek found himself thrust into a world of high stakes and even higher expectations. The notorious 100-hour work weeks were not an exaggeration; Vivek often found himself burning the midnight oil, poring over financial statements, and crafting pitch books for multi-billion dollar deals. The pressure was intense, but Vivek thrived on it, viewing each challenge as an opportunity to prove himself and expand his knowledge.

One of Vivek's early mentors at Goldman, Sarah Chen, recalls his insatiable curiosity. "Most new analysts are focused on just getting the job done," she says. "But Vivek was different. He always wanted to understand the 'why' behind every decision and every strategy. He saw the big picture in a way that was rare for someone so junior."

This curiosity served Vivek well as he navigated the complex world of investment banking. He quickly gained a reputation for his ability to synthesize vast amounts of information and distill it into clear, actionable insights. His background in science and law gave him a unique perspective on the healthcare and biotech sectors, allowing him to spot opportunities that others missed.

One particularly memorable project involved a potential merger between two pharmaceutical giants. Vivek's analysis of the companies' drug pipelines and patent portfolios proved crucial in identifying synergies that weren't immediately apparent. His work caught the attention of senior leadership, earning him a spot on more high-profile deals.

Despite his success, Vivek found himself increasingly questioning the ethics of certain practices he witnessed on Wall Street. The relentless pursuit of profit, often at the expense of broader societal benefits, didn't sit well with the idealistic young man who had entered Harvard with dreams of changing the world. He began to see his time at Goldman not as an end in itself but as a means to gain the knowledge and skills he would need to pursue his true passion: revolutionizing the healthcare industry.

After two intense years at Goldman Sachs, Vivek made the bold decision to leave the security of investment banking for the more volatile world of hedge funds. He joined QVT Financial, a multi-strategy hedge fund known for its focus on complex, value-oriented investments.

This move would prove to be a pivotal moment in Vivek's career, exposing him to a different side of finance and further honing his analytical skills.

At QVT, Vivek found himself in an environment that rewarded original thinking and contrarian views. The fund's focus on special situations and event-driven investing aligned well with Vivek's ability to spot unique opportunities, particularly in the healthcare sector. He quickly became known for his deep dives into biotech companies, often spending weeks researching a single firm's drug pipeline and market potential.

One of Vivek's colleagues at QVT, Michael Stern, remembers his unconventional approach to investment analysis. "Vivek wouldn't just look at the financials," Stern recalls. "He'd read scientific papers, talk to doctors, and even attend medical conferences. He brought a level of depth to his research that was truly impressive."

This comprehensive approach led to several successful investments for QVT. In one instance, Vivek identified a small biotech company developing a novel treatment for a rare genetic disorder. His analysis suggested that the market was significantly undervaluing the potential of the drug. QVT took a sizable position in the company, and when positive clinical trial results were announced six months later, the stock price tripled, resulting in a substantial profit for the fund.

However, Vivek's time at QVT was not without its challenges. The 2008 financial crisis hit the hedge fund industry hard, and QVT was not immune to the turmoil. Vivek found himself working around the clock to help the fund navigate the crisis, analyzing market trends and identifying opportunities amidst the chaos. This experience gave him a firsthand look at the fragility of the financial system and the far-reaching consequences of market disruptions.

Throughout his time on Wall Street, Vivek never lost sight of his broader goals. He saw his work in finance not as an end in itself but as a means to gain the knowledge, skills, and resources he would need to make a real impact in the healthcare industry. He used every opportunity to learn about the business side of biotech and pharmaceuticals, attending industry conferences and building a network of contacts in the field.

One pivotal moment came during a healthcare investment conference in San Francisco. Vivek found himself in a heated debate with the CEO of a major pharmaceutical company about the industry's approach to drug development. Vivek argued passionately for a more

50

efficient, patient-centric model that could bring lifesaving treatments to market faster and at lower cost. The CEO was dismissive, but several other attendees were intrigued by Vivek's ideas.

This encounter crystallized Vivek's vision for the future. He realized that to truly change the healthcare industry, he would need to step out of his role as an investor and take a more active role in shaping the industry's direction. He began to formulate plans for a new kind of biotech company, one that would leverage the financial and operational insights he had gained on Wall Street to revolutionize the drug development process.

As Vivek's time at QVT drew to a close, he found himself at a crossroads. He had achieved significant success in the world of finance, earning the respect of his peers and accumulating valuable experience. But he knew that his true calling lay elsewhere. The young man who had entered Harvard with dreams of changing the world was ready to take the leap from Wall Street to entrepreneurship.

Vivek's decision to leave the hedge fund world was met with surprise by many of his colleagues. He was walking away from a lucrative career at a time when most of his peers were focused on climbing the corporate ladder. But those who knew him well understood that this was a natural progression for someone with Vivek's ambition and vision.

His experiences on Wall Street had equipped him with a unique set of skills and perspectives. Goldman Sachs taught him the complexities of corporate finance and the art of deal-making. At QVT, he had honed his ability to identify undervalued assets and navigate complex market dynamics. Perhaps most importantly, he had gained a deep understanding of the financial side of the healthcare industry, knowledge that would prove invaluable in his future endeavors.

But Vivek's time in finance had also reinforced his belief that there was a better way to approach healthcare and drug development. He had seen firsthand how financial incentives often drove decision-making in the pharmaceutical industry, sometimes at the expense of patient needs. He was determined to create a new model that could balance profitability with a genuine commitment to improving human health.

As Vivek packed up his desk at QVT for the last time, he felt a mix of excitement and trepidation. He was leaving behind the security and prestige of Wall Street for the uncertain world of entrepreneurship. But he was also filled with a sense of purpose and possibility. The skills he had honed, the networks he had built, and the insights he had gained during his time in finance had prepared him for this moment.

Vivek's journey on Wall Street had been more than just a career in finance. It had been a crucible, forging his raw talent and ambition into a set of skills and perspectives that would set him apart in the business world. As he stepped out onto the streets of New York, no longer as an employee but as an entrepreneur, Vivek knew that his Wall Street experience would be the foundation upon which he would build his vision for the future of healthcare.

The lessons learned during those intense years would continue to influence Vivek's approach to business and leadership. The analytical rigor he had developed at Goldman Sachs, the contrarian thinking he had honed at QVT, and the deep understanding of the healthcare industry he had gained along the way would all play crucial roles in his future success.

Vivek's Wall Street beginnings had come to an end, but they had set the stage for the next chapter of his remarkable journey. As he looked ahead to the challenges and opportunities that awaited him in the world of biotech entrepreneurship, Vivek felt ready to take on the world. The young man from Ohio who had arrived on Wall Street with dreams of making a difference was now poised to turn those dreams into reality.

The story of Vivek Ramaswamy's time on Wall Street is more than just a tale of financial success. It's a testament to the power of perseverance, the importance of continuous learning, and the value of staying true to one's convictions. As Vivek stepped into his new role as an entrepreneur, he carried with him not just the knowledge and skills he had acquired but also a renewed sense of purpose and a clear vision for the future.

His Wall Street experience had taught him the rules of the game. He was now ready to change those rules, reshape an industry, and make a lasting impact on the world of healthcare. The next chapter of Vivek Ramaswamy's journey was about to begin, and Wall Street had given him the tools he needed to make it a success.

HIGHLIGHTS

1. Vivek's entry into Goldman Sachs' investment banking division, where he quickly distinguished himself with his unique perspective and analytical skills.

2. His ability to leverage his background in science and law to gain insights in the healthcare and biotech sectors, leading to successful deal-making.

3. Vivek's transition from Goldman Sachs to QVT Financial, where he honed his skills in complex, value-oriented investments, particularly in the biotech industry.

4. His experience navigating the 2008 financial crisis at QVT gave him valuable insights into market dynamics and financial system fragility.

QUESTIONS FOR READERS

1. How did Vivek's experiences at Goldman Sachs and QVT Financial shape his understanding of the healthcare industry?

   _____

   _____

   _____

   _____

   _____

2. What role did Vivek's background in science and law play in his success on Wall Street?

   _____

   _____

   _____

   _____

   _____

3. How might Vivek's observations of Wall Street practices have influenced his future business ethics?

_____

_____

_____

_____

_____

4. In what ways did the 2008 financial crisis impact Vivek's perspective on the financial system and his career goals?

_____

_____

_____

_____

_____

CHAPTER 5

THE BIRTH OF ROIVANT SCIENCES

==

"Innovation distinguishes between a leader and a follower." - **Steve Jobs**

==

The year was 2014, and Vivek Ramaswamy stood at the precipice of a monumental decision. His experiences on Wall Street had provided him with a unique vantage point from which to observe the pharmaceutical industry's inner workings. What he saw troubled him deeply: a system rife with inefficiencies, missed opportunities, and a focus on short-term profits over long-term patient outcomes.

Vivek's mind raced with possibilities. He envisioned a new kind of biotech company, one that could bridge the gap between the innovative potential of small research firms and the resources of big pharma. This vision would soon materialize into Roivant Sciences, a company that would reshape the world of drug development and challenge the status quo of the pharmaceutical industry.

Roivant Sciences' genesis lay in Vivek's astute observation of a critical gap in the pharmaceutical industry. Big pharma companies, burdened by bureaucracy and shareholder pressures, often shelved promising drug candidates that didn't fit their immediate strategic goals or profit margins. Meanwhile, smaller biotech firms struggled to secure the funding and expertise needed to bring their innovations to market.

Vivek saw an opportunity in this inefficiency. He believed that with the right approach, these overlooked drug candidates could be developed more efficiently, potentially bringing life-saving treatments to patients faster and at lower costs. This insight became the cornerstone of Roivant's business model.

The early days of Roivant were marked by frenetic activity. Vivek assembled a team of like-minded individuals who shared his vision and passion for revolutionizing drug development. Among them was Dr. Sarah Thompson, a brilliant pharmacologist who had grown disillusioned with traditional pharma research.

"I remember our first meeting," Dr. Thompson recalls. "Vivek laid out his vision with such clarity and conviction. He didn't just want to create another biotech company; he wanted to fundamentally change how drugs are developed and brought to market. His enthusiasm was infectious."

Vivek's approach was unconventional from the start. Instead of focusing on early-stage drug discovery, Roivant would acquire promising drug candidates that had been abandoned or deprioritized by other companies. These "dormant" assets often had significant potential but had been sidelined due to strategic decisions or financial constraints of their original developers.

The first major test of this model involved the acquisition of a compound for treating uterine fibroids. The drug had shown promise in early trials but had been shelved by its original developer. Vivek and his team saw potential where others saw risk. They acquired the rights to the compound and set about designing an innovative clinical trial program.

This approach paid off. The drug, later named Relugolix, proved highly effective in clinical trials and eventually gained FDA approval. It was a vindication of Vivek's vision and a turning point for Roivant. The success attracted attention from investors and potential partners, providing the fuel for Roivant's rapid expansion.

Vivek's leadership style during this period was a blend of visionary thinking and hands-on involvement. He was known for his ability to inspire his team with grand visions of the future while also diving deep into the minutiae of drug development and clinical trial design. This combination of big-picture thinking and attention to detail became a hallmark of Roivant's culture.

As Roivant grew, Vivek introduced another innovative concept: the "Vant" model. Instead of housing all drug development programs under one roof, Roivant would create subsidiary companies, each focused on a specific therapeutic area or technology platform. This structure allowed for more focused development efforts and attracted specialized talent and investment.

The creation of these "Vants"—companies like Axovant (neurology), Myovant (women's health and prostate cancer), and Enzyvant (rare diseases)—marked the beginning of Roivant's transformation from a single company into a biotech empire. Each Vant operated with some autonomy, but it benefited from Roivant's centralized resources and expertise.

This rapid expansion was not without its challenges. The biotech industry is notoriously risky, with high failure rates even for promising drug candidates. Vivek and his team faced skepticism from industry veterans who doubted the sustainability of Roivant's model. There were setbacks, including the failure of an Alzheimer's drug in late-stage trials, which sent shockwaves through the company and the broader biotech community.

Yet Vivek's response to these challenges revealed much about his character and leadership style. He faced the setbacks head-on, communicating transparently with investors and employees. He used these moments as opportunities for learning and refining Roivant's approach, demonstrating a resilience that inspired confidence in his team and stakeholders.

Vivek's vision extended beyond just drug development. He saw Roivant as a platform for reimagining the entire pharmaceutical value chain. This led to investments in cutting-edge technologies like artificial intelligence for drug discovery and novel approaches to clinical trial design and patient recruitment.

One of Vivek's most ambitious initiatives was the creation of Datavant, a subsidiary focused on unlocking the potential of healthcare data. Vivek recognized early on that the fragmented nature of healthcare data was a major obstacle to efficient drug development and patient care. Datavant aimed to create a secure, ethical way to link disparate healthcare datasets, potentially revolutionizing clinical research and personalized medicine.

As Roivant grew, so did Vivek's profile in the biotech world. He became known for his articulate and often contrarian views on healthcare policy and drug pricing. His appearances at industry conferences and on financial news networks made him a recognizable face of biotech innovation.

Vivek's unique background—combining expertise in science, law, and finance—allows him to navigate the complex intersection of healthcare, business, and policy with remarkable dexterity. He became an influential voice in discussions about drug pricing, healthcare reform, and the future of the pharmaceutical industry.

The rapid growth of Roivant attracted significant investment, including a landmark $1.1 billion investment from SoftBank's Vision Fund in 2017. This infusion of capital allowed Roivant to accelerate its ambitious plans, funding new drug programs and technological initiatives.

Throughout this period of explosive growth, Vivek remained focused on Roivant's core mission: bringing innovative treatments to patients more efficiently. He instilled this sense of purpose throughout the organization, creating a culture that balanced entrepreneurial spirit with scientific rigor and ethical considerations.

Dr. James Chen, a veteran pharmaceutical executive who joined Roivant in its early days, reflects on Vivek's leadership: "What struck me about Vivek was his ability to think big while never losing sight of the details. He could discuss the intricacies of a clinical trial protocol one moment and then seamlessly shift to outlining a vision for transforming the entire healthcare system the next. It's a rare combination of skills."

By 2019, just five years after its founding, Roivant had grown into a sprawling biotech empire. It encompassed over a dozen subsidiary companies, had multiple drugs in late-stage clinical trials, and had built a reputation as one of the most innovative and disruptive forces in the pharmaceutical industry.

Vivek's journey from Wall Street analyst to biotech mogul was a testament to his vision, determination, and ability to execute on bold ideas. He had identified a critical gap in the pharmaceutical industry and built a company that not only filled that gap but also challenged the fundamental assumptions of how drugs are developed and brought to market.

The story of Roivant's birth and rapid ascension is more than just a tale of business success. It's a narrative about the power of innovative thinking to drive change in an entrenched industry. Vivek Ramaswamy had not just built a successful company; he had created a new model for drug development that had the potential to accelerate the pace of medical innovation and improve patient outcomes.

As Roivant continued to grow and evolve, Vivek remained at the forefront of discussions about the future of healthcare and biotechnology. He had transformed from a Wall Street outsider to a respected industry leader, all while staying true to his original vision of creating a more efficient, patient-centric approach to drug development.

The birth of Roivant Sciences marked a pivotal chapter in Vivek Ramaswamy's journey from humble roots to business icon. It showcased his ability to identify opportunities where others saw obstacles, build and lead high-performing teams, and challenge industry norms in pursuit of a greater good.

HIGHLIGHTS

1. Vivek Ramaswamy's identification of a critical gap in the pharmaceutical industry, where promising drug candidates were often shelved by big pharma companies.

2. The innovative business model of Roivant Sciences focuses on acquiring and developing "dormant" drug assets with significant potential.

3. The creation of the "Vant" model, establishing subsidiary companies focused on specific therapeutic areas or technologies, allowed for more specialized development efforts.

4. Roivant's expansion beyond drug development into cutting-edge technologies, including the creation of Datavant to address fragmented healthcare data issues.

QUESTIONS FOR READERS

1. How did Vivek's experiences on Wall Street shape his approach to creating Roivant Sciences?

_____

_____

_____

_____

_____

2. What advantages and challenges might the "Vant" model present in drug development?

_____

_____

_____

_____

_____

3. How does Roivant's approach to acquiring "dormant" drug candidates challenge traditional pharmaceutical industry practices?

_____

_____

_____

_____

_____

4. In what ways might Vivek's leadership style have contributed to Roivant's rapid growth and success?

_____

_____

_____

_____

_____

CHAPTER 6

DISRUPTING THE PHARMACEUTICAL INDUSTRY

===

"The greatest risk is not taking any risks." In a world that's
changing quickly, the only strategy that is guaranteed to
fail is not taking risks." - **Mark Zuckerberg**

===

Vivek Ramaswamy stood before a room full of
skeptical pharmaceutical executives, his eyes
gleaming with determination. It was 2015, and
he was about to present a radical new approach to drug
development that would challenge the very foundations of
the industry. The tension in the room was palpable, but
Vivek thrived on it. He knew that to disrupt an industry as

entrenched as pharmaceuticals, he would need to be bold, innovative, and unyielding in his vision.

Roivant Sciences, under Vivek's leadership, was pioneering a new model of drug development that flew in the face of conventional wisdom. Instead of focusing on early-stage drug discovery like most biotech startups, Roivant sought to acquire promising drug candidates that had been abandoned or deprioritized by other companies. This approach was met with raised eyebrows and doubtful looks from industry veterans.

One such skeptic was Dr. Elizabeth Chen, a respected figure in pharmaceutical research. "When I first heard Vivek's pitch, I thought it was naive," she recalls. "The idea of building a company around cast-off drug candidates seemed like a recipe for failure." But as Vivek laid out his vision, explaining how Roivant would leverage advanced analytics, streamlined operations, and a nimble corporate structure to breathe new life into these overlooked assets, even the most hardened critics found themselves intrigued.

Vivek's innovative business model was built on several key pillars. First was the concept of "asset-centricity." Each drug candidate acquired by Roivant would be developed by a dedicated subsidiary company, or

"Vant," focused solely on that asset or therapeutic area. This structure allowed for more focused development efforts and attracted specialized talent and investment.

The second pillar was Roivant's unique approach to clinical trials. Vivek recognized that patient recruitment was often a major bottleneck in drug development. To address this, Roivant invested heavily in technologies to improve patient identification and engagement. They partnered with hospitals and patient advocacy groups to create a network that could quickly identify eligible participants for clinical trials.

Perhaps the most controversial aspect of Roivant's model was its aggressive use of data analytics and artificial intelligence in drug development. Vivek believed that by applying advanced computational tools to vast troves of clinical and scientific data, Roivant could make more informed decisions about which drug candidates to pursue and how to design clinical trials.

This data-driven approach led to some early successes that caught the industry's attention. In 2016, Roivant's subsidiary Axovant Sciences initiated a phase 3 trial for an Alzheimer's drug that had been abandoned by its original developer. The speed with which Axovant moved from acquiring the asset to beginning late-stage trials was unprecedented, and it generated significant buzz in the biotech world.

However, the path of disruption is never smooth, and Vivek soon faced his first major setback. In September 2017, Axovant announced that its Alzheimer's drug had failed to meet its primary endpoints in the phase 3 trial. The news sent shockwaves through the company and the broader biotech community. Roivant's stock price plummeted, and critics were quick to declare Vivek's model a failure.

It was a moment that would have broken many entrepreneurs, but Vivek's response revealed the true strength of his character. Instead of retreating or making excuses, he faced the failure head-on. In a company-wide meeting, Vivek took full responsibility for the setback and used it as a teachable moment. "We took a big swing and missed," he told his team. "But that doesn't mean we stop swinging. "It means we learn, adapt, and come back stronger."

This resilience in the face of adversity became a defining characteristic of Roivant's culture. Vivek instilled in his team the belief that failure was not something to be feared but rather an opportunity for growth and learning.

This mindset would prove crucial as Roivant continued to push the boundaries of what was possible in drug development.

Despite the Alzheimer's setback, Roivant's other ventures were showing promising results. Myovant Sciences, focused on women's health and prostate cancer, was making significant progress with its lead drug candidate. Urovant Sciences was pushing treatments for overactive bladders. These successes demonstrated the validity of Vivek's asset-centric model and helped rebuild confidence in Roivant's approach.

Vivek's disruptive vision extended beyond just drug development. He recognized that the pharmaceutical industry's challenges were systemic, involving everything from how drugs are priced to how healthcare data is managed. This led to the creation of new Roivant subsidiaries aimed at tackling these broader issues.

One of the most ambitious of these initiatives was Datavant, a company focused on breaking down data silos in healthcare. Vivek saw that the fragmented nature of healthcare data was a major obstacle to efficient drug development and patient care. Datavant aimed to create a secure, ethical way to link disparate healthcare datasets, potentially revolutionizing clinical research and personalized medicine.

This focus on data and technology set Roivant apart from traditional pharmaceutical companies. Vivek was building not just a drug development company but a technology-driven healthcare platform that could potentially transform multiple aspects of the industry.

As Roivant continued to grow and evolve, Vivek faced the challenge of scaling his disruptive vision. He needed to balance the entrepreneurial spirit that had driven Roivant's early success with the operational discipline required to manage a rapidly expanding enterprise. This led to some growing pains, including challenges in communication and coordination across the various Vant companies.

To address these issues, Vivek implemented a unique organizational structure he called "RadicalX." This model aimed to preserve the autonomy and agility of individual Vants while providing centralized support and oversight. It was a bold experiment in corporate governance, and its success or failure would have significant implications for Roivant's future.

Throughout this period of rapid growth and change, Vivek remained deeply involved in the scientific and strategic decisions of his company. He was known for his ability to dive deep into the technical details of drug development while also maintaining a broad strategic vision. This hands-on leadership style inspired confidence in his team and helped attract top talent to Roivant.

Dr. Sarah Patel, a senior scientist at one of Roivant's subsidiaries, recalls a pivotal moment that illustrated Vivek's leadership. "We were struggling with a particularly challenging aspect of our lead compound's mechanism of action," she explains. "Vivek joined one of our research meetings, and within an hour, he had not only grasped the complex scientific issues but also proposed a novel approach that we hadn't considered. His ability to quickly understand and contribute to highly technical discussions is truly remarkable."

As Roivant's profile in the industry grew, so did scrutiny of its business model and practices. Critics questioned the sustainability of Roivant's approach, arguing that the company was simply cherry-picking abandoned assets without adding real value. Others raised concerns about the ethics of Roivant's data-driven approach to drug development, fearing it might prioritize profitability over patient benefit.

Vivek met these criticisms head-on, engaging in public debates and discussions about the future of the pharmaceutical industry. He argued passionately that Roivant's model was not just about profit but about creating a more efficient system that could bring life-saving treatments to patients faster and at lower costs.

In one memorable exchange at a biotech conference, Vivek faced off against a panel of industry veterans who were skeptical of Roivant's approach. With characteristic eloquence and depth of knowledge, he not only defended his company's model but also challenged the panel to think more creatively about how to address the industry's systemic issues. His performance left a lasting impression, with many attendees remarking that they had witnessed the emergence of a new thought leader in the field.

As Roivant entered its fifth year of operation, the company had weathered significant challenges and achieved remarkable successes. It had brought multiple drugs through late-stage clinical trials, established a network of subsidiary companies tackling diverse healthcare challenges, and raised billions in investment capital. Perhaps most importantly, it has forced the pharmaceutical industry to reconsider long-held assumptions about how drugs are developed and brought to market.

Vivek's journey from Wall Street analyst to biotech disruptor was a testament to the power of innovative thinking and unwavering determination. He had identified critical inefficiencies in the pharmaceutical industry and built a company that not only addressed these issues but also challenged the fundamental assumptions of how drugs are developed and commercialized.

The story of Roivant's disruption of the pharmaceutical industry is more than just a tale of business success. It's a narrative about the potential for bold, innovative thinking to drive change in even the most entrenched industries. Vivek Ramaswamy had not just built a successful company; he had created a new paradigm for drug development that had the potential to accelerate the pace of medical innovation and improve patient outcomes worldwide.

As Roivant continued to evolve and expand its influence, Vivek remained at the forefront of discussions about the future of healthcare and biotechnology. He had transformed from an industry outsider to a respected thought leader, all while staying true to his original vision of creating a more efficient, patient-centric approach to drug development.

The disruption of the pharmaceutical industry marked a defining chapter in Vivek Ramaswamy's journey from humble roots to business icon. It showcased his ability to identify opportunities where others saw obstacles, build and lead high-performing teams, and challenge industry norms in pursuit of a greater good. As Roivant continued to push the boundaries of what was possible in biotech, it stood as a testament to Vivek's vision, determination, and unwavering commitment to improving human health.

HIGHLIGHTS

1. Roivant's innovative model of acquiring and developing abandoned drug candidates challenges traditional pharmaceutical industry practices.

2. The creation of asset-centric "Vant" subsidiaries, allowing for focused development of specific drugs or therapeutic areas.

3. Vivek's resilience in the face of setbacks, particularly his response to the Axovant Alzheimer's drug trial failure.

4. The implementation of data analytics and AI in drug development sets Roivant apart from traditional pharma companies.

QUESTIONS FOR READERS

1. How might Roivant's asset-centric model change the future of drug development and healthcare innovation?

   _____

   _____

   _____

   _____

   _____

2. What lessons can be learned from Vivek's response to the Alzheimer's drug trial failure?

   _____

   _____

   _____

   _____

   _____

3. How does Roivant's use of data analytics and AI in drug development challenge traditional pharmaceutical practices?

_____

_____

_____

_____

_____

4. In what ways does Vivek's leadership style contribute to Roivant's ability to disrupt the pharmaceutical industry?

_____

_____

_____

_____

_____

CHAPTER 7

THE ART OF LEADERSHIP

==

"Leadership is not about being in charge. It's about taking care of those in your charge." - **Simon Sinek**

==

R oivant Sciences' bustling headquarters hummed with energy as Vivek Ramaswamy strode through the open-plan office. Eyes followed him, not out of fear or pure curiosity, but with a mixture of respect and anticipation. At just 35 years old, Vivek had built a biotech empire that was reshaping the pharmaceutical industry. Yet his most remarkable achievement wasn't the company's market value or its innovative drug pipeline—it was the culture of leadership and innovation he had cultivated.

Vivek's management philosophy was as unconventional as his approach to drug development. He believed that true leadership wasn't about issuing orders from the top down but about empowering individuals at all levels to think creatively and take ownership of their work. This belief stemmed from his own experiences, from his childhood in Ohio to his time on Wall Street and his journey building Roivant.

One of Vivek's earliest leadership lessons came from an unlikely source: his high school tennis coach. "Coach Thompson never told us exactly how to play," Vivek once recalled in a company-wide meeting. "Instead, he taught us to read the game, anticipate our opponent's moves, and adapt our strategy on the fly. That's the kind of agility and strategic thinking I want to foster here at Roivant."

This philosophy manifested in Roivant's unique organizational structure. Rather than a traditional corporate hierarchy, Vivek implemented what he called a "network of networks." Each subsidiary company, or "Vant," operated with a high degree of autonomy, led by its own team of experts. Vivek's role was not to micromanage these units but to provide the vision, resources, and support they needed to succeed.

Dr. Sarah Chen, CEO of one of Roivant's subsidiary companies, described Vivek's leadership style: "He doesn't just give you a task and expect you to execute it. He challenges you to think bigger, to question assumptions, and to push the boundaries of what's possible. It's both exhilarating and demanding."

Vivek's approach to talent management was equally innovative. He believed that the key to building a world-class organization was to attract the best minds from diverse fields and create an environment where they could thrive. This meant looking beyond traditional pharma backgrounds and bringing in experts from fields like data science, artificial intelligence, and even behavioral psychology.

One of Vivek's most controversial hiring decisions was bringing on Dr. David Liu, a renowned AI researcher with no prior experience in pharmaceuticals, to lead Roivant's data science team. Many industry insiders scoffed at the idea, but Vivek saw the potential for AI to revolutionize drug discovery and development. Under Dr. Liu's leadership, Roivant developed cutting-edge algorithms that dramatically improved the efficiency of clinical trials and drug candidate selection.

Vivek's talent cultivation strategy extended beyond just hiring. He implemented a unique mentorship program where every employee, regardless of their position, was encouraged to both mentor and be mentored by others in the organization. This cross-pollination of ideas and experiences fostered a culture of continuous learning and innovation.

The program yielded unexpected benefits. In one instance, a junior lab technician's hobby in 3D printing led to a breakthrough in drug delivery mechanisms after she was paired with a senior pharmacologist in the mentorship program. Vivek often cited this as an example of the "innovation at the intersections" that he sought to encourage.

However, Vivek's leadership style was not without its challenges. His demand for excellence and rapid pace of innovation could be overwhelming for some employees. He addressed this by implementing what he called "failure"festivals"—quarterly events where team members shared their biggest mistakes and what they learned from them. These sessions not only destigmatized failure but also turned it into a valuable learning tool for the entire organization.

Vivek's commitment to fostering innovation extended beyond the walls of Roivant. He established the Roivant Foundation, which funded STEM education initiatives in underserved communities. "We're not just building a company," he often said, "we're cultivating the next generation of innovators."

The foundation's flagship program, "Science for All," brought cutting-edge lab equipment and experienced mentors to high schools across the country. Vivek personally visited many of these schools, sharing his journey from a curious teenager in Ohio to a biotech entrepreneur. His visits often left a lasting impact, inspiring students to pursue careers in science and technology.

One such student was Maria Gonzalez, now a rising star in Roivant's research division. "I met Vivek when he visited my high school in the Bronx," she recalled. "He didn't just talk about science; he talked about the power of curiosity and perseverance. It was the first time I believed that someone like me could make a difference in this field."

Vivek's leadership philosophy was put to the test during times of crisis. When one of Roivant's most promising drug candidates failed in late-stage clinical trials, the company's stock plummeted, and morale hit an all-time low. Instead of retreating to his office or making excuses, Vivek called an all-hands meeting.

"I know many of you are disappointed and worried," he began. "But I want you to remember why we're here. We're not here for the straightforward wins.

We're here to tackle the hardest problems in medicine, to push the boundaries of what's possible. Sometimes we'll fail, but each failure brings us closer to a breakthrough that could change millions of lives."

His words rallied the team. In the weeks that followed, instead of layoffs or project cancellations, Roivant saw a surge in new ideas and collaborations across departments. The crisis had become a catalyst for innovation, a testament to the resilience of the culture Vivek had built.

Vivek's approach to leadership also extended to how he interacted with competitors and critics. Rather than engaging in cutthroat competition, he sought to elevate the entire industry. He regularly spoke at conferences, sharing Roivant's successes and failures alike, in the belief that a rising tide lifts all boats.

This openness sometimes drew criticism from those who felt he was giving away competitive advantages. But Vivek stood firm. "Our mission is to improve patients' lives," he would say. "If sharing our insights helps achieve that goal faster, even if it benefits our competitors, then it's the right thing to do."

His leadership style attracted attention beyond the biotech world. Business schools began using Roivant as a case study in innovative management, and Vivek became a sought-after speaker on leadership and entrepreneurship. Yet he remained grounded, always quick to credit his team for Roivant's successes.

As Roivant continued to grow, Vivek faced the challenge of maintaining the company's innovative culture at scale. He implemented a system of "mini-Roivants" within the larger organization: small cross-functional teams with the autonomy to pursue high-risk, high-reward projects. This structure allowed Roivant to maintain the agility of a startup even as it grew into a major industry player.

Vivek's leadership philosophy was perhaps best summed up in the advice he gave to new hires: "Your job is not to have all the answers. Your job is to ask the right questions, to challenge the status quo, and to never stop learning. That's how we'll change the world."

This ethos of continuous learning and innovation permeated every aspect of Roivant's operations. From the labs where scientists were pushing the boundaries of drug discovery to the boardroom where strategic decisions were made, there was a palpable sense of purpose and possibility.

Vivek's journey from a curious child in Ohio to a transformative leader in the biotech industry is a testament to the power of visionary leadership. He didn't just build a successful company; he cultivated a culture of innovation and purpose that has the potential to reshape an entire industry.

As Roivant continues to grow and evolve, Vivek's leadership philosophy remains at its core. It's a philosophy that believes in the power of individuals to make a difference, the importance of questioning assumptions, and the transformative potential of bold ideas. It's a philosophy that has transformed a startup into a biotech powerhouse, and it continues to inspire a new generation of leaders and innovators.

The story of Vivek Ramaswamy's leadership at Roivant is more than just a tale of corporate success. It's a blueprint for how visionary leadership can drive innovation, cultivate talent, and ultimately make a positive impact on the world. As Vivek often reminds his team, "We're not just developing drugs; we're developing the future of healthcare." And under his leadership, that future looks brighter than ever.

HIGHLIGHTS

1. Vivek's "network of networks" organizational structure grants high autonomy to subsidiary companies while providing overarching vision and support.

2. The innovative talent management approach includes hiring experts from diverse fields and implementing a unique cross-level mentorship program.

3. Vivek's introduction of "failure festivals," which destigmatized mistakes and turned them into valuable learning experiences for the entire organization.

4. The establishment of the Roivant Foundation and its "Science for All" program demonstrate Vivek's commitment to fostering innovation beyond the company.

QUESTIONS FOR READERS

1. How might Vivek's "network of networks" structure be applied in other industries to foster innovation?

   _____

   _____

   _____

   _____

   _____

2. What are the potential benefits and challenges of implementing "failure festivals" in a corporate environment?

   _____

   _____

   _____

   _____

   _____

3. How does Vivek's approach to talent management and mentorship contribute to Roivant's culture of innovation?

_____

_____

_____

_____

_____

4. In what ways does Vivek's leadership during crises reflect his overall management philosophy?

_____

_____

_____

_____

_____

CHAPTER 8

GOING PUBLIC

==

"Going public is like getting married—it's easier to get in than out." - **Warren Buffett**

==

T he bustling trading floor of the New York Stock Exchange fell silent for a moment as Vivek Ramaswamy stepped up to ring the opening bell. It was June 11, 2021, and Roivant Sciences was about to make its debut as a publicly traded company. The journey to this moment had been long and fraught with challenges, but for Vivek, it represented the culmination of years of hard work, innovation, and unwavering belief in his vision.

The decision to take Roivant public had not been made lightly. Vivek had built the company from the ground up, nurturing it through its early stages and guiding it through periods of rapid growth. Now, he was preparing to share ownership with the public and subject the company to a new level of scrutiny. It was a pivotal moment in Roivant's history, as well as in Vivek's career as a business leader.

The IPO process had begun months earlier, with Vivek and his team working tirelessly to prepare the company for its public debut. They spent countless hours poring over financial statements, refining business strategies, and crafting the perfect pitch to potential investors. Vivek was determined to ensure that Roche's unique business model and innovative approach to drug development were clearly communicated and understood.

One of the biggest challenges was explaining Roivant's complex structure to potential investors. The company's network of subsidiary "Vants" was unlike anything else in the pharmaceutical industry, and Vivek knew that transparency would be key to gaining investor confidence. He personally led many of the investor presentations, using his charisma and deep knowledge of the business to address concerns and highlight opportunities.

During one particularly tense meeting with a group of skeptical institutional investors, Vivek's ability to think on his feet was put to the test. An investor challenged the viability of Roivant's model, questioning whether it was truly scalable. Without missing a beat, Vivek pulled up a series of graphs on his tablet, demonstrating how Roivant's approach had already led to faster drug development times and lower costs compared to industry averages. His quick thinking and command of the data turned the tide of the meeting, leaving the investors impressed and intrigued.

As the IPO date approached, Vivek found himself juggling the demands of the going-public process with the day-to-day operations of the company. He was determined not to let the IPO distract from Roivant's core mission of developing life-changing drugs. This meant late nights and early mornings, but Vivek's energy seemed boundless. His passion for the work and his vision for the company's future kept him going through the grueling schedule.

The night before the IPO, Vivek gathered his senior leadership team for a final pep talk. "Tomorrow, we take a huge step forward," he told them. "But remember, going public isn't the end goal. It's a means to an end. Our mission remains the same: to accelerate the development of innovative medicines and improve patients' lives. The capital we raise will fuel our work, but it's our dedication and creativity that will truly drive our success."

When the big day finally arrived, Vivek stood on the podium of the New York Stock Exchange, surrounded by his team and family. As he rang the opening bell, he couldn't help but reflect on the journey that had brought him to this moment. From his humble beginnings in Ohio to his time on Wall Street and the founding of Roivant, every experience had prepared him for this day.

The initial public offering was a resounding success. Roivant's shares opened strongly and climbed throughout the day, reflecting investor confidence in the company's innovative approach and future potential. But for Vivek, the IPO was just the beginning of a new chapter in Roivant's story.

In the weeks and months that followed, Vivek quickly learned that running a public company came with a whole new set of challenges. The quarterly earnings cycle brought intense pressure to deliver consistent results, while the increased scrutiny from analysts and shareholders meant that every decision was under the microscope.

Vivek approached these challenges with the same innovative spirit that had defined his leadership at Roivant from the beginning. He implemented a unique approach to investor relations, hosting monthly "innovation updates" in addition to the standard quarterly earnings calls. These sessions gave investors a deeper look into Roivant's drug development pipeline and technological innovations, helping to shift the focus from short-term financial metrics to long-term value creation.

One of the biggest adjustments for Vivek was balancing the demands of shareholders with his long-term vision for the company. He was determined not to fall into the trap of short-term thinking that often plagues public companies. During one contentious board meeting, where several directors were pushing for cost-cutting measures to boost short-term profits, Vivek stood his ground.

"We didn't go public to become just another pharmaceutical company focused on quarterly earnings," he argued passionately. "We went public to accelerate our mission to transform drug development." If we sacrifice long-term innovation for short-term gains, we're betraying that mission and the trust our shareholders have placed in us."

His impassioned speech won over the board, and Roivant maintained its commitment to long-term, high-impact projects. This decision would prove prescient in the coming months, as several of these projects yielded breakthrough results that significantly boosted the company's stock price and reputation.

Navigating the world of public opinion also proved to be a new challenge for Vivek. As the face of Roivant, he found himself under increased public scrutiny. Every statement he made, whether about Roivant's business or broader industry issues, was dissected and analyzed by the media and industry watchers.

Vivek embraced this new role as a public figure with characteristic enthusiasm. He saw it as an opportunity to shape the conversation around healthcare innovation and corporate responsibility. He became a regular presence on financial news networks and industry panels, using these platforms to advocate for a more patient-centric approach to drug development and a reimagining of the pharmaceutical business model.

However, this increased visibility also brought its share of controversies. When Roivant faced criticism over the price of one of its newly approved drugs, Vivek didn't shy away from the debate. Instead, he took to social media and op-ed pages to explain the company's pricing strategy and the broader issue of drug pricing in the healthcare system. His willingness to engage directly with critics and present transparent, data-driven arguments helped to diffuse the situation and even won Roivant praise for its approach to a contentious issue.

As Roivant settled into its new status as a public company, Vivek worked to maintain the innovative culture that had defined the company's early years. He was determined not to let the pressures of the public market stifle creativity or risk-taking. To achieve this, he implemented a unique incentive structure for Roivant's scientists and researchers, tying bonuses not only to financial performance but also to measures of innovation and impact.

This approach paid off in spectacular fashion when, just six months after the IPO, one of Roivant's subsidiary companies announced a major breakthrough in Alzheimer's research. The news sent Roivant's stock soaring and reaffirmed the company's position as a leader in innovative drug development.

Throughout all these challenges and triumphs, Vivek remained grounded in his original vision for Roivant. He continued to push the boundaries of what was possible in drug development, leveraging the company's newfound resources and public profile to tackle even bigger challenges in healthcare.

One year after the IPO, Vivek stood before Roivant's first annual shareholder meeting. Looking out at the sea of faces—a mix of individual investors, institutional representatives, and Roivant employees—he felt a profound sense of responsibility and excitement.

"A year ago, we made a promise," he began. "We promised to use the capital and platform provided by going public to accelerate our mission to transform drug development." Today, I'm proud to say we've not only kept that promise, but we've exceeded even our own high expectations."

He went on to outline Roivant's achievements over the past year: the breakthrough in Alzheimer's research, the launch of new subsidiary companies tackling previously overlooked diseases, and the implementation of cutting-edge AI technologies in drug discovery. But he also spoke candidly about the challenges they'd faced and the lessons learned.

"Being a public company has taught us a lot," he admitted. "It's taught us to be more transparent, more accountable, and more focused. But it hasn't changed who we are at our core. We're still the same company that believes in thinking differently, in challenging the status quo, and in never losing sight of why we do what we do— to improve patients' lives."

As he concluded his speech, Vivek reflected on how far Roivant had come since its founding. The company had grown from a small startup with a big idea to a publicly traded pharmaceutical innovator shaping the future of healthcare. But in many ways, he felt they were just getting started.

"Going public wasn't the end of our journey," he told the assembled shareholders. "It was the beginning of a new chapter. We now have the resources, the platform, and the partners to tackle the biggest challenges in healthcare. *The best is yet to come.*"

With that, Vivek stepped down from the podium, ready to lead Roivant into its next phase of growth and innovation. The IPO journey had been challenging, but it had also reaffirmed Vivek's belief in the power of bold ideas and unwavering commitment to making a difference. As he looked to the future, he was more convinced than ever that Roivant's unique approach to drug development had the potential to transform not just the pharmaceutical industry but the entire world of global healthcare.

HIGHLIGHTS

1. Vivek's personal involvement in investor presentations, effectively communicating Roivant's complex structure and innovative approach to potential investors.

2. The implementation of monthly "innovation updates" in addition to quarterly earnings calls, shifting focus from short-term financials to long-term value creation.

3. Vivek's commitment to maintaining Roivant's long-term vision and innovative culture, despite pressures for short-term gains after going public.

4. The company's successful navigation of public scrutiny and controversies, particularly regarding drug pricing, through transparent and data-driven communication.

QUESTIONS FOR READERS

1. How did Vivek's approach to investor relations differ from traditional methods, and what benefits did it bring?

_____

_____

_____

_____

_____

2. What challenges did Vivek face in balancing shareholder demands with Roivant's long-term vision?

_____

_____

_____

_____

_____

3. How did going public affect Roivant's culture of innovation, and what steps did Vivek take to preserve it?

_____

_____

_____

_____

_____

4. In what ways did Vivek's handling of public scrutiny and controversies reflect his leadership style?

_____

_____

_____

_____

_____

CHAPTER 9

BEYOND BIOTECH

==

"We need to revive the spirit of meritocracy, where the best ideas and individuals rise to the top."

- Vivek Ramaswamy

==

Vivek Ramaswamy stood at the podium, his eyes scanning the packed auditorium. The crowd, a mix of investors, industry leaders, and media, waited with bated breath. They had come expecting an announcement about Roivant's latest biotech breakthrough. Instead, Vivek was about to unveil something entirely different—a bold new venture that would take him far beyond the realm of pharmaceuticals.

"Today," he began, his voice steady and confident, "we're not here to talk about a new drug or a medical innovation. We're here to discuss a different kind of health—the health of our financial markets and the future of American capitalism."

The room fell silent. Vivek had built his reputation as a biotech wunderkind, transforming Roivant Sciences into a pharmaceutical powerhouse. Now, at the age of 37, he was setting his sights on a new horizon: the world of asset management and corporate governance.

This pivot might have seemed unexpected to some, but for those who knew Vivek well, it was a natural evolution of his restless intellect and his desire to tackle big, systemic problems. Throughout his career, Vivek had never been content to stay within the confines of any single industry or discipline. His mind was always probing, always seeking new challenges and opportunities to make an impact.

The seed for this new venture had been planted years earlier, during Vivek's time on Wall Street. He had observed firsthand the growing disconnect between corporate America and the values of everyday Americans. He saw how large asset managers, wielding enormous influence through their proxy voting power, were pushing companies to adopt policies that often seemed at odds with the interests of individual investors and the broader public good.

Vivek's new initiative, Strive Asset Management, was his answer to this problem. The company's mission was ambitious: to restore everyday citizens' voices in corporate America by offering investment products that would champion excellence over politics in boardrooms across the country.

"We're not just launching a new company," Vivek explained to the audience. "We're starting a movement to reclaim American capitalism."

The announcement sent shockwaves through the financial world. Some praised Vivek's boldness and vision, while others questioned whether a biotech entrepreneur could successfully navigate the complex world of asset management. But Vivek was no stranger to skepticism. He had faced similar doubts when he founded Roivant, and he had proven the naysayers wrong then.

In the weeks following the announcement, Vivek threw himself into building Strive with the same energy and determination that had characterized his work at Roivant. He assembled a team of experienced financial professionals, tech innovators, and policy experts.

Together, they began developing a suite of investment products that would allow everyday Americans to align their investments with their values.

One of Vivek's first hires was Sarah Chen, a veteran of the asset management industry who had become disillusioned with the status quo. "When Vivek first approached me about Strive, I was skeptical," Sarah recalled. "But the more he explained his vision, the more excited I became. Here was a chance to really change things, to make investing meaningful again."

Vivek's approach to building Strive was characteristically hands-on. He was involved in every aspect of the company's development, from crafting the investment strategy to designing the user interface for their digital platform. He spent hours in heated debates with his team, challenging assumptions and pushing for innovative solutions.

One particularly memorable brainstorming session lasted well into the night. The team was grappling with how to effectively communicate Strive's complex investment philosophy to everyday investors. Frustrated with the jargon-filled explanations they had come up with, Vivek suddenly stood up and started drawing on a whiteboard.

"Imagine you're explaining this to your grandmother," he said. "How would you make her understand why this matters?" By the end of the night, they had developed a simple, powerful message that would become the cornerstone of the Strive marketing campaign.

As Strive began to take shape, Vivek found himself navigating new and unfamiliar terrain. The regulatory world of the financial industry was vastly different from that of biotech, and he had to quickly become an expert in a whole new set of rules and regulations.

He also faced the challenge of building credibility in a field where he was seen as an outsider. Vivek tackled this head-on, embarking on a whirlwind speaking tour where he articulated his vision for Strive and engaged in spirited debates with financial industry veterans.

During one particularly heated panel discussion at a major financial conference, Vivek found himself defending Strive's approach against a group of skeptical Wall Street executives. "They argued that our model was naive, that we couldn't possibly compete with the established players," Vivek later recounted. "But I reminded them that they had said the same thing about Roivant. Innovation doesn't come from following the established playbook; it comes from rewriting the rules."

Vivek's passion and conviction won over many doubters, and Strive began to gain traction. The company's first ETF launch exceeded all expectations, attracting over $100 million in assets under management in its first week.

But Vivek's ambitions for Strive went beyond just financial success. He saw the company as a platform for reshaping the relationship between corporations and society. He began using his growing public profile to advocate for a new model of corporate governance, one that prioritized long-term value creation over short-term political expediency.

This advocacy sometimes puts Vivek at odds with powerful interests. When Strive launched a campaign challenging a major tech company's diversity policies, arguing that they were undermining meritocracy and innovation, Vivek found himself in the crosshairs of a social media firestorm.

Rather than backing down, Vivek leaned into the controversy. He penned op-eds, appeared on news shows, and engaged directly with critics on social media. His willingness to tackle contentious issues head-on earned him a reputation as a fearless truthteller, even among those who disagreed with him.

Throughout this period of intense public scrutiny, Vivek never lost sight of his ultimate goal: to build Strive into a force for positive change in the financial industry. He continued to innovate, launching new products and services designed to empower individual investors.

One of Strive's most ambitious initiatives was a platform that allowed investors to directly influence the proxy voting decisions of the companies they invested in. This technology, which Vivek dubbed "democracy dollars," had the potential to fundamentally reshape corporate governance.

"For too long, a handful of asset managers have wielded enormous influence over corporate America," Vivek explained at the launch event. "With Democracy Dollars, we're putting that power back in the hands of everyday investors."

The launch of Democracy Dollars was a turning point for Strive. It catapulted the company from an intriguing upstart to a genuine disruptive force in the financial industry. Major institutional investors began to take notice, and some even started to adopt elements of Strive's approach.

As Strive grew, Vivek found himself increasingly in demand as a thought leader on corporate governance and responsible capitalism. He was invited to testify before Congress, speak at the World Economic Forum, and advise government officials on financial policy.

Through it all, Vivek remained grounded in his original vision for Strive. He was determined to build a company that would outlast him, one that would continue to champion the interests of everyday investors long after he was gone.

This long-term thinking was reflected in Strive's corporate structure. Vivek implemented a unique governance model that enshrinked the company's mission in its charter and created safeguards against short-term profit-seeking at the expense of that mission.

"We're building Strive for the long haul," Vivek told his team during a company-wide meeting. "Our goal isn't just to be successful in the market—it's to change the market itself."

Three years after its launch, Strive had grown into a formidable player in the asset management industry. It had over $10 billion in assets under management, a suite of popular ETFs, and a reputation for challenging the status quo.

But for Vivek, this was just the beginning. He saw Strive as part of a larger movement to redefine the role of business in society. He began to speak and write more broadly about the need for a new model of capitalism, one that balanced profit with purpose and prioritized long-term value creation over short-term gains.

Vivek's broader vision led him to explore new ventures beyond Strive and Roivant. He became involved in initiatives ranging from education reform to technology ethics, always bringing his unique blend of entrepreneurial spirit and philosophical inquiry to bear on complex societal challenges.

One such venture was a nonprofit organization dedicated to promoting civic education and engagement among young Americans. Vivek saw this as a natural extension of Strive's mission, recognizing that an informed and engaged citizenry was crucial to the health of both democracy and capitalism.

"We can't expect people to be responsible investors if they don't understand the basic principles of how our economic and political systems work," Vivek explained at the launch of the initiative. "This is about building the foundation for a more robust and resilient form of capitalism."

As Vivek's influence grew, so did the scrutiny he faced. Critics accused him of overreach, arguing that he was straying too far from his area of expertise. Others questioned his motives, suggesting that his forays into politics and social issues were driven by personal ambition rather than genuine conviction.

Vivek met these criticisms head-on, engaging in public debates and continuing to articulate his vision for a more responsible and inclusive form of capitalism. He remained committed to his belief that business leaders had a responsibility to engage with broader societal issues.

"The challenges we face as a society are too big and too complex to be solved by the government alone," he argued in a widely shared op-ed. "Business has a crucial role to play, not just in creating wealth but in shaping the kind of society we want to live in."

As Vivek looked to the future, he saw endless possibilities. Strive was just the beginning—a proof of concept for a new way of thinking about the role of business and finance in society. He envisioned a network of interconnected ventures, each tackling a different aspect of the challenges facing modern capitalism.

"We're not just building companies," Vivek told a group of young entrepreneurs at a conference. "We're building a movement. A movement to reclaim the promise of American capitalism and to ensure that it serves the interests of all Americans, not just a privileged few."

With Strive firmly established and new ventures on the horizon, Vivek Ramaswamy had truly moved beyond biotech. He had transformed himself from a pharmaceutical entrepreneur into a leading voice on the future of capitalism. And in doing so, he had opened up a new chapter in his journey from humble roots to greatness.

HIGHLIGHTS

1. Vivek's bold expansion beyond biotech with the launch of Strive Asset Management, aiming to restore the voice of everyday citizens in corporate America.

2. The development of "Democracy Dollars," a platform allowing investors to directly influence proxy voting decisions, reshaping corporate governance.

3. Vivek's hands-on approach in building Strive, from crafting investment strategies to engaging in public debates about the company's mission.

4. The rapid growth of Strive to $10 billion in assets under management within three years, establishing itself as a disruptive force in the financial industry.

QUESTIONS FOR READERS

1. How might Vivek's experience in biotech have influenced his approach to disrupting the asset management industry?

2. What potential impacts could Strive "Democracy Dollars" have on corporate governance and shareholder activism?

3. How does Vivek's expansion into various ventures reflect his vision for the role of business in society?

_____

_____

_____

_____

_____

4. What challenges might Vivek face in balancing his diverse interests while maintaining credibility in each field?

_____

_____

_____

_____

_____

CHAPTER 10

THE OUTSPOKEN EXECUTIVE

===

"The most courageous act is still to think for yourself aloud." - **Coco Chanel**

===

Vivek Ramaswamy stood before the cameras with a relaxed posture but intense eyes. The bright studio lights illuminated his features as he prepared to address millions of viewers on one of the nation's most-watched news programs. This wasn't his first time in the spotlight, but tonight was different. Tonight, he was about to ignite a firestorm of controversy that would reverberate through corporate boardrooms across America.

"Corporate wokeness," Vivek began, his voice clear and steady, "is not just a distraction from the core mission of businesses. It's a dangerous ideology that threatens the very foundations of American capitalism." The host leaned forward, intrigued by the boldness of the statement. For the next hour, Vivek laid out his case against what he saw as the growing trend of corporations prioritizing political and social agendas over their primary responsibilities to shareholders and customers.

This appearance marked a turning point in Vivek's public persona. No longer content to be seen solely as a biotech innovator or a maverick investor, he was now positioning himself as a vocal critic of what he perceived as the excesses of corporate America's embrace of progressive politics.

Vivek's journey to this moment had been anything but conventional. Born to immigrant parents in Ohio, he had risen through the ranks of Wall Street before founding Roivant Sciences and disrupting the pharmaceutical industry. However, it was his experiences as a CEO and his observations of the changing corporate world that led him to this new battleground.

The seeds of Vivek's crusade against corporate wokeness were sown during his time at Roivant. He had watched with growing concern as companies across various industries began to take public stances on controversial social and political issues. While many praised these moves as socially responsible, Vivek saw them as a dangerous distraction from the core purpose of business.

"Companies are not elected officials," he would often say. "They don't have the mandate to make broad societal decisions. Their job is to create value for their shareholders and customers, not to push a political agenda."

Vivek's views were shaped by his unique perspective as both an insider and an outsider in corporate America. As a successful CEO, he understood the pressures faced by executives to conform to prevailing social trends. But as the son of immigrants who had achieved success through hard work and merit, he also saw the potential dangers of policies that prioritized identity over ability.

His first major foray into this debate came in the form of an op-ed in The Wall Street Journal. Titled "Why I Won't Hire Based on Race," the piece argued against the growing trend of corporate diversity initiatives that Vivek saw as thinly veiled racial quotas. The article sparked immediate controversy, with praise and criticism pouring in from all corners.

Rather than shy away from the backlash, Vivek leaned into it. He began accepting invitations to speak on news programs, podcasts, and at conferences. His message remained consistent: American businesses needed to refocus on their core missions and leave politics to the political sphere.

Vivek's media appearances were characterized by his unique blend of intellect and charisma. He had a knack for breaking down complex issues into digestible soundbites without oversimplifying them. Whether debating seasoned political pundits or explaining his views to late-night talk show hosts, Vivek always seemed to be in his element.

One particularly memorable exchange occurred during a panel discussion at a prestigious business school. When challenged by a student about the responsibility of businesses to address social issues, Vivek responded with a question of his own: "If we expect corporations to solve our societal problems, what role is left for democratic governance? Are we comfortable ceding that much power to unelected business leaders?"

The question left the auditorium in thoughtful silence, demonstrating Vivek's ability to reframe debates and challenge conventional wisdom.

As Vivek's public profile grew, so did the intensity of the reactions to his views. He became a lightning rod for both praise and criticism. Supporters hailed him as a brave voice of reason in an increasingly polarized corporate world. Critics accused him of being out of touch or even actively harmful to progress.

Through it all, Vivek remained undeterred. He viewed the controversy as a necessary part of sparking a broader conversation about the role of business in society. "If everyone agrees with you," he often said, "you're probably not saying anything worth saying."

Vivek's crusade against corporate wokeness wasn't limited to media appearances and public speaking. He put his money where his mouth was, using his position as CEO of Roivant Sciences and later as the founder of Strive Asset Management to implement policies that aligned with his views.

At Roivant, he instituted a strict policy of political neutrality, forbidding the company from taking stands on issues not directly related to its business. At Strive, he went even further, creating investment products specifically designed to pressure companies to focus on financial performance rather than social or political agendas.

These actions drew both admiration and ire from different quarters of the business world. Some praised Vivek for having the courage to stand by his convictions, while others accused him of using his platforms to push his own political agenda.

Vivek's response to such criticisms was characteristically direct. "I'm not pushing an agenda," he would argue. "I'm pushing for the absence of agendas in spaces where they don't belong. Business should be about business, not politics."

As Vivek's public profile grew, so did the demands on his time. He found himself juggling his responsibilities as a CEO with an increasingly busy schedule of media appearances, speaking engagements, and writing commitments. It was a balance act that required incredible discipline and energy.

A typical day might see Vivek starting with a 5 AM workout, followed by a series of meetings with Roivant executives, a lunchtime interview with a major newspaper, an afternoon of work on his latest book, and an evening appearance on a cable news show. Through it all, he maintained a level of focus and articulation that left many wondering how he managed it.

The answer, according to those close to him, lay in Vivek's unwavering commitment to his principles and his belief in the importance of the conversation he was sparking. "Vivek doesn't see this as a distraction from his work," explained Sarah Chen, a longtime colleague. "He considers it essential to his mission to improve business."

Vivek's outspokenness on corporate issues soon led to him being sought out for commentary on a wide range of topics. He became a go-to voice for discussions on everything from healthcare policy to tech regulation to geopolitics. While some questioned whether he was stretching himself too thin, Vivek saw these opportunities as a chance to bring his unique perspective to a broader audience.

One of Vivek's most impactful media appearances came during a heated debate on a popular political talk show. The subject was the role of big tech companies in moderating online speech. While other panelists argued for either stricter or looser regulations, Vivek proposed a novel solution that would treat social media platforms as common carriers, similar to telephone companies.

His argument, delivered with his trademark blend of historical context and forward-thinking analysis, shifted the entire conversation. In the days that followed, Vivek's proposal was discussed and debated in policy circles, demonstrating his ability to influence public discourse far beyond the business world.

As Vivek's public profile grew, so did interest in his personal story. Journalists and biographers sought to understand the experiences that had shaped his worldview. Vivek was generally private about his personal life, but he did open up about the influence of his immigrant parents and his upbringing in Ohio.

He spoke of how his parents had instilled in him a deep appreciation for the opportunities America offered, along with a strong work ethic and a belief in the power of education. These values, he explained, formed the foundation of his views on meritocracy and his skepticism of identity-based policies.

Vivek's rise as a public intellectual wasn't without its challenges. His growing media presence's demands sometimes clashed with his responsibilities as CEO. There were occasions when board members or investors expressed concern that his outspokenness might negatively impact the company's image or bottom line.

But Vivek remained convinced that his public advocacy was not just compatible with his role as a business leader but essential to it. He argued that by speaking out on issues affecting the broader business world, he was helping to create an environment in which companies like Roivant could thrive.

"My job as CEO isn't just to manage the company within the existing system," he would explain. "It's to help shape the system in ways that allow for true innovation and value creation."

As Vivek's influence grew, so did calls for him to enter politics. Supporters argued that his unique blend of business acumen and political insight would make him an ideal candidate for high office. Vivek, however, remained noncommittal, insisting that he could have a greater impact as an independent voice in the private sector.

Whether he would eventually heed the call of public service remained to be seen, but one thing was clear: Vivek Ramaswamy had established himself as one of the most distinctive and influential voices in American public life. From the boardroom to the TV studio, he had demonstrated an unwavering commitment to speaking his mind and challenging the status quo.

As this chapter in Vivek's life unfolded, it became clear that his journey from a young entrepreneur to a leading voice in national debates was far from over. With each media appearance and public statement, he was not just sharing his views but shaping the conversation about the future of American business and society.

The outspoken executive from Ohio had become a force to be reckoned with, his voice echoing far beyond the corridors of corporate America.

HIGHLIGHTS

1. Vivek's bold stance against "corporate wokeness" and his argument that businesses should focus on their core missions rather than political agendas.

2. His impactful Wall Street Journal op-ed "Why I Won't Hire Based on Race," which sparked widespread debate on corporate diversity initiatives.

3. Vivek's implementation of political neutrality at Roivant Sciences and the creation of politically neutral investment products at Strive Asset Management.

4. His ability to influence public discourse beyond the business world is exemplified by his novel proposal for regulating social media platforms as common carriers.

QUESTIONS FOR READERS

1. How might Vivek's background as a CEO and entrepreneur influence his views on corporate social responsibility?

   _____

   _____

   _____

   _____

   _____

2. What potential impacts could Vivek's stance against "corporate wokeness" have on the broader business world?

   _____

   _____

   _____

   _____

   _____

3. How does Vivek's approach to public discourse challenge traditional notions of a CEO's role?

_____

_____

_____

_____

_____

4. In what ways might Vivek's outspokenness on various issues influence public perception of his companies and personal brand?

_____

_____

_____

_____

_____

CHAPTER 11

WRITING AND THOUGHT LEADERSHIP

===

"The pen is mightier than the sword."

- Edward Bulwer-Lytton

===

Vivek Ramaswamy sat at his desk, fingers poised over the keyboard, ready to ignite a firestorm. The clock on his computer read 2:37 AM, but sleep was the furthest thing from his mind. He was about to write the opening lines of what would become one of the most controversial and influential books of the decade: "Woke, Inc.: Inside Corporate America's Social Justice Scam."

The journey to this moment had been a long one, filled with late-night discussions, heated debates, and a growing conviction that something was fundamentally wrong with the direction of modern capitalism. Vivek had always been a voracious reader and a passionate debater, but it wasn't until he found himself at the helm of a major biotech company that he truly began to grapple with the complexities of corporate America's relationship with society.

His experiences as CEO of Roivant Sciences had given him a front-row seat to what he saw as a disturbing trend: corporations increasingly abandoning their core missions in favor of virtue signaling and political posturing. What started as occasional observations soon became a burning desire to speak out, to challenge the prevailing wisdom, and to offer a different vision for the role of business in society.

The idea for "Woke, Inc." had been percolating in Vivek's mind for months. He had been jotting down notes, collecting anecdotes, and refining his arguments through countless conversations with friends, colleagues, and even critics. Now, finally, he was ready to put it all together in a coherent narrative that he hoped would shake the foundations of corporate America.

As Vivek began to write, the words flowed like a torrent. He wrote about the dangers of stakeholder capitalism, arguing that it allowed CEOs to pursue their own political agendas under the guise of social responsibility. He steppedd into the history of corporate purpose, tracing how the modern conception of socially conscious business had evolved and where, in his opinion, it had gone off track.

But "Woke, Inc." wasn't just a critique. Vivek was determined to offer solutions, to chart a path forward that would allow businesses to be both profitable and socially beneficial without becoming de facto political actors. He drew on his background in biotech, his experiences on Wall Street, and his deep knowledge of history and philosophy to craft a nuanced argument for a new kind of capitalism.

The writing process was intense. Vivek would often work through the night, fueled by a combination of passion and caffeine. His wife, Apoorva, would sometimes find him asleep at his desk in the morning, his face illuminated by the glow of his computer screen. She worried about the toll this project was taking on him, but she also understood its importance to him.

"This isn't just a book," Vivek explained to her one evening. "It's a manifesto. It's a call to action for business leaders to remember their true purpose and to resist the temptation to become pseudo-governments."

As news of Vivek's book project spread, it generated both excitement and trepidation in business circles. Some CEOs privately reached out to express their support, sharing their own frustrations with the pressures to conform to certain political stances. Others were wary, concerned that Vivek's book might upset the delicate balance they had struck between various stakeholder groups.

The manuscript of "Woke, Inc." landed on publishers' desks like a bombshell. Bidding wars erupted as publishing houses recognized the potential of Vivek's provocative thesis. Eventually, a major publisher secured the rights, promising a massive promotional campaign to match the book's ambitions.

In the months leading up to the book's release, Vivek embarked on a grueling schedule of interviews, podcast appearances, and speaking engagements. He was determined to ensure that "Woke, Inc." wasn't just another business book that would be quickly forgotten. He wanted to start a movement to change the conversation about the role of business in society.

The day of the book's release brought a flurry of media attention. "Woke, Inc." debuted at the top of bestseller lists, its provocative title and Vivek's growing public profile ensuring widespread interest. But it wasn't just the sales figures that mattered to Vivek. He was more interested in the conversations being started in the book.

Reactions to "Woke, Inc." were as diverse as they were passionate. Business leaders, politicians, academics, and everyday readers all weighed in. Some hailed it as a much-needed wake-up call, a bold challenge to the excesses of stakeholder capitalism. Others criticized it as a defense of an outdated, profit-at-all-costs mentality.

Vivek relished the debate. He appeared on countless talk shows, engaged in spirited discussions on social media, and participated in public forums to defend and explain his ideas. His background as a successful entrepreneur gave him credibility in business circles, while his eloquence and deep knowledge of history and philosophy allowed him to hold his own against academic critics.

One particularly memorable exchange occurred during a panel discussion at a prestigious university. A professor of business ethics challenged Vivek, arguing that his ideas would lead to a return to the robber baron era of unrestrained capitalism. Vivek's response was characteristically nuanced and thought-provoking.

"The choice isn't between soulless profit-seeking and virtue-signaling stakeholder capitalism," he argued. "There's a third way. Businesses can focus on their core missions, create value for shareholders, and benefit society without becoming political actors. It's about doing what you do best and doing it ethically, not about trying to solve every social problem."

The influence of "Woke, Inc." extended far beyond the business world. Politicians on both sides of the aisle found themselves grappling with Vivek's ideas. Conservative thinkers embraced his critique of corporate wokeness, while some progressive leaders were forced to reconsider their approach to corporate regulation in light of his arguments.

Vivek's book also sparked a renewed interest in the history and philosophy of capitalism. Reading groups and college courses began to incorporate "Woke, Inc." into their curricula, using it as a launching point for discussions about the proper role of business in society.

As the impact of "Woke, Inc." continued to ripple through society, Vivek found himself increasingly in demand as a thought leader. He was invited to speak at major conferences, contribute to leading publications, and advise policymakers on issues related to corporate governance and economic policy.

But with this greater influence came increased scrutiny. Critics began to dig into Vivek's own business practices, looking for inconsistencies between his written words and his actions as CEO. Vivek welcomed this scrutiny, seeing it as an opportunity to demonstrate the practicality of his ideas.

He pointed to Roivant's focus on its core mission of developing life-saving drugs, its refusal to take political stances unrelated to its business, and its merit-based hiring practices as examples of his philosophy in action. While not everyone was convinced, many observers were impressed by Vivek's willingness to practice what he preached.

The success of "Woke, Inc." led to calls for Vivek to write more, to expand on his ideas and address new challenges facing the business world. He began work on a follow-up book, this time focusing on the intersection of technology, democracy, and capitalism.

As Vivek's reputation as a thought leader grew, so did his influence on a new generation of entrepreneurs and business leaders. Young CEOs reached out to him for advice, citing "Woke, Inc." as a formative influence on their approach to business. Business schools began inviting him to speak, eager to expose their students to his challenging ideas.

One young entrepreneur, Sarah Chen, credited Vivek's book with changing the course of her career. "Reading 'Woke, Inc.' made me realize that I could build a successful company without compromising my values or becoming a political actor," she said. "It gave me the courage to focus on creating real value rather than chasing the latest social trends."

Vivek's ideas also began to influence policy discussions. Lawmakers and regulators started to question the wisdom of pushing corporations to take on roles traditionally reserved for government. Debates about corporate social responsibility took on new dimensions, with Vivek's arguments providing a fresh perspective.

Throughout this period of intense public engagement, Vivek never lost sight of his roots or the experiences that had shaped his worldview. He often spoke of his parents' immigrant journey, the values they had instilled in him, and how these influences had informed his critique of modern capitalism.

"My parents came to this country with nothing but their skills and their willingness to work hard," he would say. "They succeeded because America provided them with opportunities, not because corporations assumed the role of government. We need to preserve that system of opportunity, not replace it with a form of corporate feudalism."

As "Woke, Inc." approached its first anniversary, its impact was undeniable. It had changed the conversation about corporate purpose, challenged prevailing notions of stakeholder capitalism, and established Vivek Ramaswamy as one of the leading business thinkers of his generation.

But for Vivek, this was just the beginning. He saw "Woke, Inc." not as the end of a journey but as the start of a new chapter in his life's work. He was determined to continue writing, speaking, and advocating for a vision of capitalism that balanced profit with purpose and innovation with responsibility.

"Writing 'Woke, Inc.' taught me the power of ideas," Vivek reflected in a quiet moment. "It showed me that one book, one argument, can change the way people think about fundamental issues. That's a responsibility I take very seriously, and it's one that will guide my work for years to come."

As Vivek looked to the future, he saw endless possibilities for continuing to shape the debate about the role of business in society. Whether through more books, public speaking, or direct engagement with business and political leaders, he was committed to advancing his vision of a more focused, more effective form of capitalism.

The journey from biotech entrepreneur to bestselling author and thought leader had been an unexpected one for Vivek Ramaswamy. But it was a role he had grown to embrace, recognizing the unique platform it gave him to influence the future of American capitalism. As he sat down to begin work on his next book, Vivek felt a sense of excitement and purpose. The conversation he had started with "Woke, Inc." was far from over, and he was eager to see where it would lead next.

HIGHLIGHTS

1. Vivek Ramaswamy's writing of "Woke, Inc.: Inside Corporate America's Social Justice Scam," a critique of modern stakeholder capitalism and corporate political activism.

2. The book's immediate impact upon release, sparking widespread debate among business leaders, politicians, academics, and the general public.

3. Vivek's engagement in numerous public discussions and media appearances to defend and explain his ideas, showcasing his ability to articulate complex concepts.

4. The influence of "Woke, Inc." on policy discussions, causing lawmakers and regulators to reconsider approaches to corporate social responsibility.

141

QUESTIONS FOR READERS

1. How might Vivek's personal background and experiences as a CEO have shaped the arguments presented in "Woke, Inc."?

_____

_____

_____

_____

_____

2. What potential long-term impacts could Vivek's critique of stakeholder capitalism have on corporate governance and policy?

_____

_____

_____

_____

_____

3. How does Vivek's approach to thought leadership challenge traditional notions of a business leader's role in society?

_____

_____

_____

_____

_____

4. In what ways might the ideas presented in "Woke, Inc." influence future generations of entrepreneurs and business leaders?

_____

_____

_____

_____

_____

CHAPTER 12

PERSONAL LIFE AND VALUES

===

"The greatest legacy one can pass on to one's children and grandchildren is not money or other material things accumulated in one's life, but rather a legacy of character and faith." **- Billy Graham**

===

Vivek Ramaswamy sat on the porch of his Cincinnati home on a quiet Sunday morning, cradling his newborn son. The world knew him as a biotech mogul, a Wall Street prodigy, and a vocal critic of corporate America. But in this moment, he was simply a father, marveling at the tiny life in his arms and contemplating the values he hoped to instill in his child.

For all his public persona and professional accomplishments, Vivek's personal life remained a sanctuary, grounded in the principles and relationships that had shaped him from his earliest days. The son of Indian immigrants, Vivek had grown up in a household that prized education, hard work, and cultural heritage. These values, instilled by his parents, had been the bedrock of his success and continued to guide him as he navigated the complexities of his adult life.

Vivek's relationship with his wife, Apoorva, was a testament to the balance he strived to maintain between his professional ambitions and personal beliefs. They had met during their undergraduate years at Harvard, bonding over shared interests in philosophy and public policy. Apoorva, a Yale Law School graduate and accomplished physician in her own right, was Vivek's intellectual equal and strongest supporter.

Their partnership was built on mutual respect and shared values. Apoorva understood the demands of Vivek's career, having witnessed his meteoric rise from Wall Street analyst to biotech entrepreneur. She provided a grounding influence, reminding him of the importance of family and personal integrity amidst the whirlwind of his professional life.

One of the couple's favorite rituals was their weekly "idea dinners," where they would discuss everything from the latest developments in healthcare policy to ancient philosophy. These conversations often sparked new insights for Vivek, influencing his business decisions and public positions. Apoorva was not just a supportive spouse but a trusted advisor and intellectual sparring partner.

The arrival of their children brought a new dimension to Vivek's life. Known for his intense focus and tireless work ethic, he now found himself learning to balance the demands of his career with the joys and responsibilities of fatherhood. He was determined to be a present and engaged parent, drawing inspiration from his own father's example.

Vivek's approach to parenting reflected his broader philosophy on life and success. He believed in setting high expectations while providing unwavering support. He and Apoorva made a conscious effort to create a home environment that valued curiosity, critical thinking, and moral character above material success.

This emphasis on values extended to Vivek's professional life, too. Despite the pressures of running a multibillion-dollar company and maintaining a high public profile, he remained committed to the principles that had

146

guided him from the start. He was known for his unwavering ethical stance, often making difficult business decisions based on his personal convictions rather than expediency.

One such incident occurred early in his tenure as CEO of Roivant Sciences. Faced with the opportunity to fast-track a potentially lucrative drug by cutting corners on safety protocols, Vivek chose the longer, more expensive route. "I couldn't look my children in the eye if I compromised on something so fundamental," he explained to his board of directors. This decision, while initially controversial, ultimately enhanced the company's reputation for integrity.

Vivek's commitment to his beliefs sometimes puts him at odds with prevailing trends in corporate America. His outspoken criticism of what he termed "woke capitalism" drew both praise and criticism. Yet, even his detractors acknowledged his consistency in applying his principles to both his personal and professional life.

The Ramaswamy household was a blend of cultures and traditions. Vivek and Apoorva made a conscious effort to instill in their children an appreciation for their Indian heritage while embracing their American identity. Holidays were a mix of Diwali celebrations and Thanksgiving dinners, reflecting the family's multicultural background.

Language was an important part of this cultural preservation. Vivek, fluent in Tamil thanks to his parents' insistence, made sure his children were exposed to the language from an early age. He often recited Tamil poetry to them, explaining the deep philosophical concepts embedded in the ancient verses.

Despite his busy schedule, Vivek prioritized family time. He had a strict rule of being home for dinner at least four nights a week, barring extraordinary circumstances. These family dinners were a time for connection and conversation, where topics ranged from school activities to global affairs. Vivek believed in engaging his children in substantive discussions from an early age, encouraging them to form and articulate their own opinions.

The Ramaswamys were also committed to community service, a value they actively instilled in their children. They regularly volunteered at local shelters and participated in community events. Vivek often spoke about the importance of giving back, citing his own family's journey from humble beginnings to success as a reason for their commitment to helping others.

Balancing his professional ambitions with his personal beliefs and family commitments was an ongoing challenge for Vivek. There were times when the demands of his career threatened to overwhelm his personal life. During the intense period of writing "Woke, Inc.," for instance, Vivek found himself working long into the night, sometimes missing family dinners and bedtime stories.

Apoorva was the one who helped him recalibrate. "Your words will have more impact if they come from a place of balance and personal fulfillment," she reminded him. This gentle nudge led Vivek to reassess his priorities and make changes to his work habits. He began to schedule his writing time more efficiently, ensuring it didn't encroach on family time.

Vivek's public persona as a fierce critic of corporate America sometimes created challenges in his personal relationships. Some longtime friends, uncomfortable with his outspoken views, distanced themselves. Yet Vivek remained true to his convictions, believing that honest disagreement was preferable to superficial harmony.

He and Apoorva made a point of maintaining friendships with people across the political spectrum, often hosting dinners where lively debates were encouraged. These gatherings reflected Vivek's belief in the importance of civil discourse and the exchange of ideas and values he hoped to pass on to his children.

As his professional responsibilities grew, Vivek became increasingly intentional about carving out time for personal growth and reflection. He maintained a disciplined routine of early morning meditation and exercise, practices he credited with helping him stay grounded amidst the pressures of his public life.

Vivek also made time for his lifelong passion for classical piano. Music had been a significant part of his life since childhood, and he found that it provided a necessary counterbalance to the analytical thinking required in his business and writing endeavors. He often said that some of his best ideas came to him while he was playing Bach or Beethoven.

The Ramaswamy family's commitment to education extended beyond their own children. Vivek and Apoorva were active supporters of educational initiatives in underserved communities, believing that access to quality education was key to unlocking individual potential and driving societal progress.

They established a scholarship fund for first-generation college students, inspired by their own parents' immigrant journeys.

Vivek often mentored these students, sharing not just his professional expertise but also the life lessons he had learned about maintaining personal integrity in the face of professional pressures.

As Vivek's public profile grew, he became increasingly aware of the impact his actions and words could have on his family. He was protective of his children's privacy, carefully managing his public image to shield them from undue attention. At the same time, he was open with them about his work and the principles he stood for, hoping to lead by example.

One of Vivek's greatest challenges was reconciling his critique of stakeholder capitalism with his desire to create positive change in the world. He grappled with questions of how to be a socially responsible business leader without falling into the traps he had identified in "Woke, Inc."

His solution was to focus on excellence in his core business while supporting causes he believed in through personal philanthropy. This approach allowed him to maintain the integrity of his business practices while still contributing to social good in a way that aligned with his personal values.

As he looked to the future, Vivek was acutely aware of the legacy he wanted to leave, both for his family and for society at large. He often spoke of his desire to contribute to a renewal of American values, emphasizing personal responsibility, meritocracy, and freedom of thought.

"I want my children to inherit a world where ideas are debated openly, where merit is rewarded, and where individuals are free to pursue their dreams," he once said in an interview. "But more than that, I want them to inherit a set of values that will guide them through life's challenges."

For Vivek Ramaswamy, the pursuit of professional success was inextricably linked to his personal values and family commitments. His journey from humble beginnings to business icon was not just a story of individual achievement but a testament to the power of principled living and the enduring influence of family and cultural heritage.

As he continued to navigate the complex worlds of business, politics, and public discourse, Vivek remained anchored by the relationships and beliefs that had shaped him. In the end, he measured his success not just by his professional accomplishments but also by his ability to live out his values and positively influence the lives of others, starting with his own family.

The story of Vivek Ramaswamy's personal life and values is a reminder that even in the highest echelons of business and public life, it is our core principles and relationships that define us. It is a narrative that continues to unfold, shaped by a man's daily choices and interactions, striving to balance ambition with integrity and public influence with personal fulfillment.

HIGHLIGHTS

1. Vivek's strong partnership with his wife Apoorva, including their weekly "idea dinners," influenced his business decisions and public stances.

2. His commitment to balancing professional demands with engaged fatherhood, emphasizing curiosity, critical thinking, and moral character in his children's upbringing.

3. The Ramaswamy family's effort to blend Indian heritage with American identity, including language preservation and cultural celebrations.

4. Vivek's dedication to community service and education initiatives, including establishing a scholarship fund for first-generation college students.

QUESTIONS FOR READERS

1. How do Vivek's personal values influence his approach to business and public life?

   _____

   _____

   _____

   _____

   _____

2. In what ways does Vivek balance his professional ambitions with his family commitments?

   _____

   _____

   _____

   _____

   _____

3. How does the Ramaswamy family's multicultural background shape their parenting and lifestyle choices?

_____

_____

_____

_____

_____

4. What challenges might Vivek face in maintaining his personal beliefs while navigating the corporate world?

_____

_____

_____

_____

_____

CHAPTER 13

CONTROVERSIES AND CRITICISMS

==

"To avoid criticism, say nothing, do nothing, be nothing."

– Aristotle

==

Vivek Ramaswamy stood at the podium, his posture relaxed but his eyes intense. The room was filled with journalists, industry peers, and curious onlookers, all eager to hear his response to the latest wave of criticism that had crashed upon his shores. It was a familiar scene for the outspoken entrepreneur, who had become as known for his controversial stances as for his business acumen.

The journey from a young biotech innovator to a lightning rod for public debate had been a swift one for Vivek. His rapid rise in the pharmaceutical industry, coupled with his vocal criticism of corporate America, had thrust him into the spotlight and under the microscope. Every decision, every statement, and every business move was now subject to intense scrutiny.

One of the earliest controversies Vivek faced centered around Roivant Sciences' business model. Critics argued that the company's strategy of acquiring abandoned drug candidates from other firms was more financial engineering than true innovation. They painted Vivek as a Wall Street shark in scientist's clothing, more interested in quick profits than in advancing medical science.

Vivek's response to these criticisms was characteristic of his approach to public scrutiny. Rather than becoming defensive or retreating from the public eye, he leaned into the debate. He embarked on a media tour, appearing on financial news networks, writing op-eds, and engaging in public forums to explain and defend Roivant's model.

"We're not just picking up other companies' leftovers," Vivek argued during one particularly heated television interview. "We're identifying promising compounds that have been abandoned for reasons that often have nothing to do with their medical potential. We're giving these drugs a second chance to help patients."

His passionate defense and clear articulation of Roivant's mission won over many skeptics. However, it also raised his profile further, making him an even bigger target for criticism.

The publication of "Woke, Inc." marked a turning point in Vivek's public persona. His scathing critique of stakeholder capitalism and corporate social justice initiatives ignited a firestorm of controversy. Supporters hailed him as a brave truthteller, while detractors accused him of promoting a regressive and narrow view of corporate responsibility.

One particularly pointed criticism came from a group of prominent business school professors, who published an open letter arguing that Vivek's ideas were dangerous and out of touch with modern economic realities. They claimed that his emphasis on shareholder primacy ignored the complex web of stakeholders that modern corporations must consider.

Vivek didn't shy away from this challenge. Instead, he invited his critics to a public debate at a major university. The event, which was live streamed to a global audience, became a seminal moment in the ongoing discussion about the purpose of the corporation in society.

During the debate, Vivek demonstrated his intellectual agility and deep knowledge of corporate history and economics. He argued passionately that the trend towards stakeholder capitalism was not just misguided but actively harmful to both businesses and society at large.

"When we ask corporations to solve all of society's problems, we're abdicating our responsibilities as citizens and ceding too much power to unelected business leaders," he contended. "We need to refocus corporations on their core missions and address social issues through democratic processes."

While the debate didn't settle the issue, it did elevate the discussion and cement Vivek's reputation as a formidable intellectual force. Even those who disagreed with him had to respect his willingness to engage in open and rigorous debate.

However, the controversy surrounding Vivek wasn't limited to his public statements and writings. His business practices at Roivant and later at Strive Asset Management also came under intense scrutiny.

One particularly thorny issue arose when a drug developed by one of Roivant's subsidiaries failed in late-stage clinical trials. The company's stock price plummeted, and critics accused Vivek of overhyping the drug's potential. Some even suggested that he had misled investors about the likelihood of the drug's success.

Vivek responded to these accusations with characteristic transparency. He held a press conference where he walked through the data from the clinical trials, explaining in detail why the company had been optimistic about the drug's prospects and what they had learned from its failure.

"In the world of drug development, failure is always a possibility," he explained. "What matters is how we respond to failure and what we learn from it. We remain committed to our mission of bringing life-saving treatments to patients, and we will continue to pursue that mission with integrity and transparency."

This approach to addressing criticism head-on, with facts and reasoned arguments, became a hallmark of Vivek's public persona. He never shied away from a debate, whether it was about his business practices or his political views.

One of the most persistent criticisms Vivek faced was the accusation that he was using his businesses as a platform to advance his personal political agenda. This charge intensified with the launch of Strive Asset Management, which explicitly positioned itself as a counterweight to the ESG (Environmental, Social, and Governance) movement in investing.

Critics argued that Vivek was hypocritical, criticizing other business leaders for mixing business and politics while doing the same thing himself. They pointed to his media appearances, his book, and his public statements as evidence that he was more interested in pushing a political ideology than in running successful businesses.

Vivek's response to this criticism was nuanced. He argued that there was a fundamental difference between using a business as a platform for political activism and building a business around a clear set of principles and values.

"What we're doing at Strive is not about pushing a political agenda," he explained in a widely-shared LinkedIn post. *"It's about offering investors a choice. We believe that companies should focus on excellence in their core businesses rather than trying to solve every social problem. That's not a political stance—it's a business philosophy."*

This explanation didn't satisfy all of his critics, but it did resonate with many in the business community who shared his concerns about the expanding scope of corporate activism.

Throughout all these controversies, Vivek maintained a remarkable level of composure and focus. He seemed to thrive on the intellectual challenge of defending his ideas and actions. However, the constant scrutiny and criticism did take a toll on his personal life.

In a rare moment of vulnerability during a podcast interview, Vivek admitted that the public battles had sometimes strained his relationships with family and friends. "It's not easy being at the center of these debates," he said. "But I believe deeply in the importance of these issues, and I feel a responsibility to speak out, even when it's difficult."

This sense of mission and purpose seemed to sustain Vivek through even the most intense periods of criticism. He frequently spoke of his parents, who had faced their own challenges as immigrants building a new life in America. Their resilience and determination in the face of adversity had instilled in Vivek a deep well of strength that he drew upon in his public battles.

Despite the controversies, or perhaps because of them, Vivek's influence in the business world continued to grow. His willingness to tackle difficult issues head-on and engage in substantive debates earned him respect even from those who disagreed with him.

One of Vivek's most vocal critics, a prominent journalist who had written several critical pieces about him, later admitted in an interview, "I may not agree with everything Vivek says, but I respect his intellectual honesty and his willingness to engage in real dialogue. He's forcing us to grapple with important questions about the role of business in society."

This ability to elevate the discourse and bring important issues to the forefront became one of Vivek's most significant contributions to the business world. Even as he faced criticism and controversy, he was shaping the conversation about corporate purpose, stakeholder capitalism, and the relationship between business and society.

Throughout it all, Vivek remained committed to his core principles and his vision for a more focused, more effective form of capitalism. He continued to write, speak, and build businesses that reflected these values, undeterred by the criticism and controversy that swirled around him.

The story of Vivek Ramaswamy's journey through controversy and criticism is ultimately a testament to the power of conviction and the importance of engaging in open, honest debate. From a young entrepreneur facing skepticism about his business model to an influential voice challenging the orthodoxies of modern capitalism, Vivek demonstrated that true leadership often means being willing to stand firm in the face of criticism and to engage thoughtfully with one's critics.

HIGHLIGHTS

1. Vivek's proactive approach to addressing criticisms about Roivant Sciences' business model involves engaging in media tours and public forums to explain and defend the company's strategy.

2. The controversial impact of "Woke, Inc." and Vivek's willingness to participate in public debates, such as the live streamed event with business school professors.

3. Vivek's transparent response to the failure of a drug in late-stage clinical trials, holding a press conference to explain the data and reaffirm the company's commitment to its mission.

4. The launch of Strive Asset Management and Vivek's defense against accusations of using his businesses as a platform for personal political agendas.

QUESTIONS FOR READERS

1. How does Vivek's approach to addressing public criticism reflect his leadership style and personal values?

_____

_____

_____

_____

_____

2. In what ways might Vivek's willingness to engage in public debates about controversial issues impact his businesses and personal brand?

_____

_____

_____

_____

_____

3. How does Vivek balance transparency and protection of business interests when responding to criticisms about company setbacks?

_____

_____

_____

_____

_____

4. What potential long-term effects could Vivek's controversial stances have on his influence in the business world and public discourse?

_____

_____

_____

_____

_____

CHAPTER 14

VISION FOR AMERICAN CAPITALISM

==

"The business of business should be business."

- Milton Friedman

==

Vivek Ramaswamy stood before a packed auditorium at the Harvard Business School, his alma mater. The audience, a mix of eager students, skeptical professors, and curious industry leaders, waited with bated breath. They had come to hear Vivek's much-anticipated lecture on his vision for the future of American capitalism. As he began to speak, it was clear that this would be no ordinary business talk.

"For too long," Vivek began, his voice resonating with conviction, "we've allowed the concept of stakeholder capitalism to distort the fundamental purpose of business in society. Today, I want to challenge this prevailing wisdom and propose a new paradigm for American capitalism—one that returns to first principles while addressing the unique challenges of our time."

This opening salvo set the tone for what would become a defining moment in Vivek's career as a thought leader. Over the next two hours, he laid out a comprehensive vision for reshaping American capitalism, drawing on his experiences as a biotech entrepreneur, his studies of economic history, and his deep-seated belief in the power of free markets to drive innovation and prosperity.

Central to Vivek's vision was a redefinition of stakeholder responsibility. He argued that the current interpretation of stakeholder capitalism, which calls on businesses to balance the interests of shareholders, employees, customers, communities, and the environment, was fundamentally flawed. In Vivek's view, this approach diluted corporate focus, reduced accountability, and ultimately harmed the very stakeholders it purported to serve.

"When a business tries to be all things to all people," he explained, "it ends up being nothing to anyone. We need to return to a model in which businesses focus on their core missions, creating value for customers and returns for shareholders. This doesn't mean ignoring other stakeholders, but rather recognizing that the best way to serve them is through excellence in the business's primary function."

To illustrate his point, Vivek drew examples from his own career. He recounted how Roivant Sciences, by focusing intensely on its mission of developing life-saving drugs, had ultimately created more value for all stakeholders than if it had diverted resources to unrelated social initiatives. "By succeeding in our core mission," he said, "we created jobs, advanced medical science, and generated returns that could be reinvested in further innovation. That's how business can truly benefit society."

But Vivek's vision went beyond just critiquing stakeholder capitalism. He proposed a new economic paradigm that he called "excellence capitalism." This model would prioritize meritocracy, innovation, and long-term value creation over short-term profit maximization or political appeasement.

"Excellence capitalism," Vivek explained, "is about unleashing the full potential of human creativity and enterprise. It's about creating an environment where the best ideas can flourish, regardless of where they come from. It's about rewarding genuine value creation rather than financial engineering or political maneuvering."

This concept resonated strongly with many in the audience, particularly the students who were grappling with their own career choices and ethical dilemmas. One student, Sarah Chen, later recalled, "Vivek's ideas challenged everything we'd been taught about corporate social responsibility. It was compelling to see businesses focus on being the best at what they do rather than solving every social problem."

Vivek went on to outline specific policy proposals to support his vision of excellence in capitalism. He advocated for reforms to corporate governance laws, changes to the tax code to incentivize long-term investment, and an overhaul of regulations that he saw as stifling innovation. He also called for a renewed emphasis on STEM education and immigration policies that would attract the world's top talent to American shores.

Throughout his lecture, Vivek was careful to address potential criticisms of his ideas. He acknowledged the genuine concerns that had led to the rise of stakeholder capitalism, such as income inequality and environmental degradation. He argued, however, that these issues were better addressed through democratic processes and targeted

172

government policies than by expanding the role of corporations.

"We shouldn't ask businesses to be pseudo-governments," he said. "That's a recipe for unaccountable power and reduced economic dynamism. Instead, we should empower our democratic institutions to address social issues while allowing businesses to focus on what they do best—creating value through goods and services."

The reaction to Vivek's lecture was immediate and polarized. Some in the audience were energized by his vision, seeing it as a needed corrective to what they viewed as the excesses of stakeholder capitalism. Others were skeptical, arguing that Vivek's ideas were a throwback to a less socially conscious era of business.

One particularly heated moment came during the Q&A session when a professor challenged Vivek on the environmental implications of his vision. "How can we trust businesses to act responsibly if they're only focused on their bottom line?" the professor demanded.

Vivek's response was characteristically nuanced. "Environmental responsibility isn't separate from the bottom line—it's integral to it," he argued. "A business that depletes natural resources or alienates its community is not creating long-term value. Excellence capitalism isn't about ignoring these factors; it's about addressing them in a way that aligns with the business's core competencies and creates sustainable value."

This exchange highlighted one of the key strengths of Vivek's approach—his ability to engage thoughtfully with critics and to find common ground even in areas of disagreement. His ideas resonated with even skeptics due to this trait.

In the weeks and months following the Harvard lecture, Vivek's vision for American capitalism became a topic of intense debate in business schools, boardrooms, and policy circles across the country. He was invited to speak at conferences, write op-eds for major publications, and testify before congressional committees.

One particularly significant moment came when Vivek was asked to present his ideas at the World Economic Forum in Davos. Standing before a global audience of business and political leaders, he made a powerful case for excellence in capitalism as a model not just for America but for the world.

"The challenges we face—from climate change to income inequality to technological disruption—are global in nature," he told the Davos audience. "They require a global response. But that response should be rooted in unleashing human potential and fostering innovation, not in constraining business or centralizing control."

As Vivek's ideas gained prominence, they began to influence real-world business practices and policy discussions. Several major corporations announced plans to refocus on their core competencies and move away from unrelated social initiatives. Policymakers began to explore ways to incentivize long-term value creation and promote innovation.

However, Vivek's vision also faced significant challenges. Critics argued that his model didn't adequately address pressing social and environmental issues. Some accused him of promoting a form of capitalism that was too narrowly focused on shareholder returns.

Vivek met these criticisms head-on, engaging in public debates and continually refining his ideas. He emphasized that excellence capitalism was not about ignoring social responsibility but about redefining how businesses could best contribute to society.

"The most socially responsible thing a business can do," he often said, "is to excel at its core mission. A pharmaceutical company that develops life-saving drugs, a tech company that creates transformative products, a bank that efficiently allocates capital—these are the real engines of social progress."

As his ideas continued to evolve, Vivek began to explore ways to put them into practice on a larger scale. He launched initiatives to promote entrepreneurship and innovation, particularly in underserved communities. He worked with policymakers to develop proposals for regulatory reform that would foster a more dynamic and competitive business environment.

One of Vivek's most ambitious projects was the creation of an "Excellence Index," a new way of measuring corporate performance that went beyond traditional financial metrics. This index took into account factors like innovation output, long-term value creation, and alignment with core competencies. Several major investors began to incorporate the Excellence Index into their decision-making processes, signaling a potential shift in how corporate success was evaluated.

Throughout this period of intense activity and public scrutiny, Vivek remained grounded in the values and experiences that had shaped his worldview. He often spoke of his parents' immigrant journey and the opportunities that American capitalism had provided for his family. This personal connection to the power of free enterprise gave his arguments an authenticity and passion that resonated with many.

As Vivek's vision for American capitalism continued to gain traction, he remained acutely aware of the challenges ahead. He knew that transforming deeply entrenched systems and mindsets would be a long-term project, requiring persistence, flexibility, and a willingness to engage with diverse perspectives.

"This isn't about returning to some idealized past," he would often say. "It's about forging a new path forward—one that harnesses the innovative power of capitalism while addressing the unique challenges of our time. It's a vision of capitalism that's true to its roots but adapted for the 21st century."

Vivek Ramaswamy's journey from biotech entrepreneur to influential economic thinker was far from over. But with his vision for excellence in capitalism, he had staked out a bold position in the ongoing debate about the future of American business and society. Whether his ideas would ultimately reshape American capitalism remained to be seen, but there was no doubt that he had changed the conversation in profound and lasting ways.

HIGHLIGHTS

1. Vivek's introduction of "excellence capitalism" as a new economic paradigm, prioritizing meritocracy, innovation, and long-term value creation over short-term profit maximization or political appeasement.

2. His critique of stakeholder capitalism, arguing that it dilutes corporate focus and ultimately harms the stakeholders it aims to serve.

3. Vivek's proposal for specific policy reforms, including changes to corporate governance laws, tax code modifications, and regulatory overhauls to support his vision of excellence capitalism.

4. The creation of the "Excellence Index," a new metric for measuring corporate performance beyond traditional financial indicators.

QUESTIONS FOR READERS

1. How might Vivek's concept of "excellence capitalism" address or fall short in tackling current social and environmental issues?

_____

_____

_____

_____

_____

2. In what ways could focusing on core competencies, as Vivek suggests, lead to greater innovation and societal benefit?

_____

_____

_____

_____

_____

3. How does Vivek's background as an immigrant and entrepreneur influence his vision for American capitalism?

_____

_____

_____

_____

_____

4. What potential challenges might arise in implementing Vivek's ideas on a large scale across diverse industries and economies?

_____

_____

_____

_____

_____

CHAPTER 15

THE GLOBAL STAGE

==

"The world is a book, and those who do not travel read only one page." - **Saint Augustine**

==

Vivek Ramaswamy stood at the podium in the grand conference hall of the World Economic Forum in Davos, Switzerland. The room was filled with global leaders, influential economists, and titans of industry from every corner of the world. As he surveyed the audience, Vivek couldn't help but reflect on the journey that had brought him to this moment—from a young immigrant's son in Ohio to a voice shaping global economic discourse.

His speech that day would mark a pivotal moment in Vivek's career, catapulting him onto the international stage and solidifying his reputation as a thought leader in global business. But the road to Davos had been long and filled with challenges, triumphs, and unexpected turns.

Vivek's foray into international business began almost by accident. In the early days of Roivant Sciences, he had focused primarily on the U.S. market, seeing it as the epicenter of pharmaceutical innovation. However, a chance meeting with a Japanese pharmaceutical executive at a conference in Boston opened his eyes to the untapped potential of global markets.

The executive, Dr. Hiroshi Tanaka, was intrigued by Roivant's innovative approach to drug development. Over dinner, he shared insights into the unique challenges and opportunities in the Japanese pharmaceutical market. Vivek listened intently, his mind racing with possibilities.

Within months of that meeting, Roivant had established a Japanese subsidiary, partnering with local firms to navigate the complex regulatory world. This move not only opened up new revenue streams but also provided access to a wealth of scientific talent and novel compounds that had been overlooked by Western companies.

Roivant's success with the Japanese venture sparked a period of rapid global expansion. Vivek crisscrossed the globe, from the biotech hubs of Europe to the emerging markets of India and China. Each new market presented its own set of challenges, but Vivek approached them with the same blend of intellectual curiosity and strategic thinking that had defined his career.

In Europe, Roivant faced skepticism from regulators who were wary of the company's unconventional business model. Undeterred, Vivek personally led a series of presentations to regulatory bodies, explaining how Roivant's approach could actually accelerate the development of much-needed treatments. His persuasive arguments and deep understanding of both the scientific and business aspects of drug development won over many skeptics.

The expansion into India was particularly meaningful for Vivek. Although he had been born and raised in the United States, his Indian heritage had always been an important part of his identity. He was now bringing cutting-edge biotechnology to his ancestors' country, potentially improving millions of lives.

During a visit to a research facility in Bangalore, Vivek met a young scientist named Priya Patel. She shared with him her frustration at the lack of resources for developing treatments for diseases that primarily affected the developing world. Inspired by her passion, Vivek initiated a new Roivant subsidiary focused specifically on neglected tropical diseases. This move not only filled a crucial gap in global health but also demonstrated Vivek's commitment to using business as a force for positive change on a global scale.

As Roivant's international footprint grew, so did Vivek's reputation as a global business leader. He was increasingly invited to speak at international conferences and contribute to global economic discussions. His unique perspective—combining Western business acumen with an understanding of emerging markets—made him a valuable voice in debates about the future of global capitalism.

One particularly memorable moment came during a panel discussion at the Asia-Pacific Economic Cooperation (APEC) summit. The topic was innovation's role in driving economic growth, and Vivek found himself sharing the stage with government ministers and CEOs from all over the region. When asked about the challenges of fostering innovation in diverse economic systems, Vivek delivered an impassioned speech about the importance of creating ecosystems that encourage risk-taking and reward creativity.

"Innovation isn't just about technology or R&D spending," he argued. "It's about creating a culture that values new ideas and is willing to challenge the status quo.

This is true whether you're in Silicon Valley, Shanghai, London, or Lagos."

His words resonate strongly with the audience, and in the following weeks, several APEC member countries reached out to Vivek for advice on shaping their innovation policies. This experience opened Vivek's eyes to the potential impact he could have beyond the business world, shaping economic policy on a global scale.

However, Vivek's growing international influence also brought new challenges and criticisms. Some accused him of exporting a particularly American brand of capitalism that might not be suitable for all cultures and economic systems. Others questioned whether a pharmaceutical executive should have such a significant voice in broader economic discussions.

Vivek addressed these criticisms head-on, often engaging in public debates with his detractors. He argued that while his ideas were shaped by his American experience, they were fundamentally about unleashing human potential—a goal that transcended national boundaries. He also pointed out that his firsthand experience in building a global business gave him unique insights into the challenges and opportunities of the modern economy.

One of Vivek's most significant contributions to global economic discussions was his concept of "glocalization," a strategy that combined global reach with local adaptation. He argued that successful international businesses needed to balance universal principles with sensitivity to local cultures and markets.

This idea was put to the test when Roivant entered the Chinese market. The company faced significant cultural and regulatory hurdles, and initial progress was slow. Rather than forcing a one-size-fits-all approach, Vivek empowered the local team to adapt Roivant's model to the Chinese context. This flexibility paid off, and within two years, the Chinese subsidiary had become one of Roivant's fastest-growing units.

Vivek's experiences in China also led him to become a vocal advocate for intellectual property rights on the global stage. He argued that strong IP protections were crucial for encouraging innovation and investment, particularly in the knowledge-based industries that were increasingly driving global economic growth.

During a high-profile debate at the World Trade Organization, Vivek made a compelling case for harmonizing IP laws across countries. "In a world where ideas are the most valuable currency," he said, "we need a global system that protects and rewards innovation while ensuring that the benefits are shared widely."

His arguments influenced ongoing trade negotiations and helped shape the intellectual property provisions in several international agreements. This experience further cemented Vivek's role as a bridge builder between the business world and the realm of international policy.

As Vivek's global influence grew, he never lost sight of his roots or the values that had shaped his worldview. He often spoke about how his immigrant background had given him a unique perspective on global issues, allowing him to see connections and opportunities that others might miss.

This perspective was evident in Vivek's approach to talent management at Roivant's international subsidiaries. He implemented a robust exchange program, allowing employees from different countries to work in other global offices. This not only facilitated knowledge transfer but also helped create a truly global corporate culture.

During a visit to Roivant's London office, Vivek met with a group of employees who had participated in the exchange program. One young researcher, originally from Brazil, shared how her experience working in the Tokyo office had completely changed her approach to problem-solving. "I learned that there's never just one right way to do things," she said. "Now, I always try to look at challenges from multiple cultural perspectives."

Vivek was deeply moved by this feedback. It reinforced his belief that diversity of thought and experience was a key driver of innovation and success in the global economy. He began to incorporate these ideas more explicitly into his public speeches and writings, arguing for a more interconnected and culturally fluent approach to international business.

As Vivek's international profile continued to rise, he found himself increasingly in demand as an advisor to governments and international organizations. He was appointed to several high-level advisory boards, including a UN committee on sustainable development and a World Bank initiative on fostering entrepreneurship in developing countries.

These roles allowed Vivek to influence global economic policy at the highest levels. He advocated for policies that would encourage innovation, protect intellectual property, and create opportunities for entrepreneurs around the world. His unique blend of business acumen and policy insight made him a valuable voice in discussions about how to navigate the challenges of the 21st-century global economy.

One of Vivek's most ambitious projects was the creation of a global innovation index. This index went beyond traditional economic metrics to measure factors like educational quality, regulatory environment, and cultural attitudes towards risk-taking. The index quickly became a valuable tool for policymakers and investors, providing insights into the innovation potential of different countries and regions.

As Vivek stood at the podium in Davos, preparing to deliver his speech, he reflected on the journey that had brought him to this moment. From his early days as a biotech entrepreneur to his current role as a global thought leader, he had remained committed to his core values of innovation, meritocracy, and using business as a force for positive change.

His speech that day would outline his vision for a new era of global capitalism—one that balanced competition with cooperation, profit with purpose, and global reach with local relevance. As he began to speak, the room fell silent, with the world's leaders leaning in to hear the ideas of the man who had risen from humble roots to reshape the global economic conversation.

189

Vivek's journey to the global stage was far from over. But as he stood before the world's elite, sharing his vision for the future of international business and economics, it was clear that his voice would continue to shape global discussions for years to come. The immigrant's son from Ohio had truly become a citizen of the world, using his unique perspective and relentless drive to push for a more innovative, inclusive, and prosperous global economy.

HIGHLIGHTS

1. Vivek's expansion of Roivant Sciences into international markets, starting with Japan and extending to Europe, India, and China, demonstrates his ability to adapt to diverse business environments.

2. The establishment of a Roivant subsidiary focused on neglected tropical diseases, showcasing Vivek's commitment to addressing global health challenges through business.

3. Vivek's introduction of the concept of "glocalization"—balancing g global reach with local adaptation—proved successful in entering challenging markets like China.

4. His influential role in global economic discussions, particularly in areas such as intellectual property rights and innovation policy, impacts international agreements and negotiations.

QUESTIONS FOR READERS

1. How has Vivek's immigrant background influenced his approach to global business expansion and economic discussions?

   _____

   _____

   _____

   _____

   _____

2. In what ways might Vivek's concept of "glocalization" be applied to other industries beyond pharmaceuticals?

   _____

   _____

   _____

   _____

   _____

3. How does Vivek's advocacy for intellectual
   property rights on the global stage reflect his views
   on innovation and economic growth?

   _____

   _____

   _____

   _____

   _____

4. What potential long-term impacts could Vivek's
   global innovation index have on international
   economic policy and business strategies?

   _____

   _____

   _____

   _____

   _____

CHAPTER 16

THE MAKING OF A LEGACY

==

"The future belongs to those who believe in the beauty of their dreams." - **Eleanor Roosevelt**

==

Vivek Ramaswamy stood at the podium, his gaze sweeping across the eager faces of the graduating class before him. The commencement address he was about to deliver at his alma mater, Harvard University, was more than just a celebration of academic achievement. It was a moment of reflection on the journey that had brought him here and the legacy he was in the process of creating.

As he began to speak, Vivek's mind wandered to the early days of Roivant Sciences. As a young, ambitious entrepreneur, he entered a pharmaceutical industry that was vastly different from the one that exists today. His innovative approach to drug development, once met with skepticism, had become a model for companies around the world.

Roivant's impact on the pharmaceutical industry was undeniable. The company's strategy of reviving abandoned drug candidates had not only led to the development of life-saving treatments, but also forced Big Pharma to reassess its approach to research and development. Vivek's insistence on transparency and data sharing had helped break down silos within the industry, fostering a more collaborative approach to drug discovery.

One of Roivant's most significant contributions was the development of a groundbreaking treatment for a rare genetic disorder. The drug, which had been abandoned by its original developer due to market size concerns, was given new life under Vivek's leadership. Its success not only transformed patients' lives, but also demonstrated the viability of Roivant's model.

Dr. Sarah Chen, a leading geneticist who had worked on the project, later remarked, "Vivek's approach showed us that with the right combination of scientific rigor and entrepreneurial spirit, we could tackle diseases that the industry had previously deemed too risky or unprofitable."

This success's ripple effects extended far beyond Roivant. Other companies began to adopt similar strategies, leading to a renaissance in drug development for rare diseases. Vivek's vision had not just changed one company; it had shifted the entire industry's paradigm.

But Vivek's impact wasn't limited to the realm of pharmaceuticals. His outspoken criticism of corporate culture and his advocacy for a new model of capitalism had made him a polarizing figure in the business world. Yet, even his critics couldn't deny the influence he wielded.

Vivek's book, "Woke, Inc.," had ignited a national conversation about the role of corporations in society. His arguments against stakeholder capitalism and in favor of a more focused approach to business had resonated with many, particularly younger entrepreneurs who were disillusioned with traditional corporate models.

One such entrepreneur was Michael Torres, the founder of a successful tech startup. "Reading Vivek's book was a turning point for me," Torres said in an interview. "It gave me permission to focus on building a fantastic product without feeling guilty about not solving every social problem. That focus is what allowed us to innovate and ultimately create more value for society."

Vivek's ideas had also begun to shape business education. Leading business schools had incorporated his concepts into their curricula, sparking debates about corporate purpose and responsibility. The "Ramaswamy Framework," as it came to be known, became a standard tool for analyzing business ethics and strategy.

However, Vivek's legacy was not without controversy. His critics argued that his emphasis on shareholder value and corporate focus could lead to a neglect of important social and environmental concerns. These debates often played out in public forums, with Vivek always willing to engage in spirited discussion.

One particularly memorable exchange occurred during a televised debate with a prominent advocate of stakeholder capitalism. When challenged on the social responsibility of corporations, Vivek responded with characteristic eloquence: "The most socially responsible thing a business can do is to excel at its core mission. A pharmaceutical company that develops life-saving drugs, a tech company that creates transformative products—these are the real engines of social progress."

This ability to articulate complex ideas in compelling ways was a key part of Vivek's influence. He had a talent for distilling intricate business and economic concepts into language that resonated with a broad audience. This skill had made him a sought-after speaker and commentator, further amplifying his impact on public discourse.

Vivek's influence also extended to the political realm. While he never ran for office himself, his ideas shaped policy debates on issues ranging from corporate regulation to innovation policy. He frequently testified before congressional committees, offering insights on how to foster a more dynamic and competitive business environment.

One of Vivek's most significant policy contributions was his work on patent reform. Drawing on his experiences in the pharmaceutical industry, he advocated for changes that would protect innovation while preventing abuse of the patent system. His proposals formed the basis for legislation that reshaped the intellectual property world in the United States.

As Vivek continued his commencement address, he reflected on the challenges that lay ahead for the next generation of business leaders. He spoke of the need for ethical leadership, the importance of long-term thinking, and the potential for business to be a force for positive change in the world.

"Your generation," he told the graduates, "has the opportunity to redefine what business success looks like. It's not just about profits or stock prices. It's about creating real value, solving real problems, and leaving the world better than you found it."

These words encapsulated the core of Vivek's legacy—a vision of business that was both pragmatic and idealistic, focused yet socially conscious. It was a legacy still in the making, with its full impact yet to be realized.

The influence of Vivek's ideas was already evident in the changing practices of major corporations. Companies were beginning to reassess their corporate social responsibility programs, focusing on initiatives that aligned more closely with their core competencies. This shift led to more effective and sustainable forms of corporate impact.

In the pharmaceutical industry, Vivek's legacy was particularly pronounced. The model he had pioneered at Roivant had become a blueprint for a new generation of biotech companies. These firms were characterized by their agility, their willingness to take on high-risk projects, and their innovative approaches to drug development.

Dr. James Lee, a veteran pharmaceutical executive, observed, "Vivek showed us that there was another way to do things. He proved that you could be both profitable and innovative, that you could take on projects the big companies had abandoned and turn them into successes. That's changed the whole world of drug development."

But perhaps the most significant aspect of Vivek's legacy was his impact on young entrepreneurs. His story—from the son of immigrants to a business icon—had inspired countless individuals to pursue their own entrepreneurial dreams. Vivek had become a role model for a new generation of business leaders who sought to combine commercial success with a strong ethical foundation.

This influence was evident in the rise of what some called "Ramaswamy-style" startups—companies characterized by their laser focus on core competencies, their emphasis on meritocracy, and their commitment to creating genuine value. These firms were proving that Vivek's ideas could translate into successful business practices across various industries.

As he concluded his commencement address, Vivek offered a final piece of advice to the graduates: "Don't be afraid to challenge conventional wisdom. The greatest innovations, the most transformative ideas, often come from those willing to question the status quo. Your unique perspectives and experiences are your greatest assets. Use them to shape the future of American business."

The applause that followed was more than just a polite response to a commencement speaker. It was a recognition of Vivek's already significant impact and the potential for his ideas to continue shaping the business world for years to come.

As Vivek left the stage, he knew that his work was far from over. The legacy he was creating was not a static achievement but an ongoing process. There were still challenges to overcome, ideas to refine, and battles to fight in the realm of business and public policy.

Yet, as he looked out at the sea of young faces before him, Vivek felt a sense of optimism. He saw in these graduates the potential to take his ideas further, to build upon his legacy and create their own. The future of American business, he realized, was in positive hands.

Vivek's journey from a young entrepreneur with a bold idea to a figure shaping the future of American capitalism was a testament to the power of vision, perseverance, and principled leadership. His legacy, still in the making, promised to influence the worlds of business, policy, and innovation for generations to come.

As he left the Harvard campus that day, Vivek's mind was already turning to the next challenge, the next idea, the next opportunity to make a difference. For him, legacy was not about resting on past achievements but about continuing to push forward, to innovate, and to inspire. The next chapter of his story and of American business was yet to be written.

HIGHLIGHTS

1. Vivek's innovative approach to drug development at Roivant Sciences, which transformed the pharmaceutical industry's paradigm, especially in the realm of rare disease treatments.

2. The widespread impact of Vivek's book "Woke, Inc." on national conversations about corporate culture and the role of businesses in society.

3. The incorporation of Vivek's ideas into business school curricula led to the development of the "Ramaswamy Framework" for analyzing business ethics and strategy.

4. Vivek's influence on policy debates, particularly his work on patent reform, reshaped the intellectual property world in the United States.

QUESTIONS FOR READERS

1. How might Vivek's approach to pharmaceutical development influence future innovations in healthcare and other industries?

   _____

   _____

   _____

   _____

   _____

2. In what ways could the "Ramaswamy Framework" shape the next generation of business leaders and their decision-making processes

   _____

   _____

   _____

   _____

   _____

3. How does Vivek's legacy challenge traditional notions of corporate social responsibility and business ethics?

_____

_____

_____

_____

_____

4. What potential long-term impacts could "Ramaswamy-style" startups have on the American business world and economy?

_____

_____

_____

_____

_____

EPILOGUE

Vivek Ramaswamy's journey from the son of immigrants to a transformative figure in American business is a testament to the enduring power of the American Dream. His story embodies the ideals of innovation, determination, and principled leadership that have long defined the nation's entrepreneurial spirit.

From his early days as a precocious student in Ohio to his meteoric rise in the pharmaceutical industry, Vivek consistently demonstrated an ability to see opportunities where others saw obstacles. His founding of Roivant Sciences revolutionized drug development, breathing new life into abandoned compounds and bringing hope to patients with rare diseases.

But Vivek's impact extends far beyond the realm of pharmaceuticals. His vocal criticism of corporate culture and his advocacy for a new model of capitalism have sparked crucial debates about the role of business in society. Through his writings, speeches, and media appearances, he has challenged conventional wisdom and inspired a new generation of entrepreneurs to think differently about success and social responsibility.

Perhaps most remarkably, Vivek has achieved all this while staying true to his core values and beliefs. His unwavering commitment to meritocracy, innovation, and ethical leadership has set a new standard for business leaders in the 21st century.

Yet Vivek's story is far from over. His ongoing work continues to shape the future of American business and public policy. From his efforts to reform patent laws to his advocacy for a more focused approach to corporate governance, Vivek remains at the forefront of some of the most pressing issues facing the business world today.

As we reflect on Vivek's meteoric rise, it's clear that his greatest legacy may be the inspiration he provides to others. His journey proves that with vision, hard work, and unwavering principles, it's possible to not just succeed in business but to fundamentally change entire industries and shape public discourse.

Vivek Ramaswamy's story is a reminder of the transformative power of ideas and the impact that one individual can have when they dare to challenge the status quo.

EXCLUSIVE BONUS

SCAN THIS CODE
TO GET YOUR
BONUS GIFT

EXTRA BONUSES

10+ EXTRA DIGITAL BIOGRAPHY BOOKS FOR YOU!

Thank you for choosing our book!

Visit our Instagram and Facebook page to download all the extra bonuses now!

Scan the QR code to join the group:

@EDUVERSITYPRESS

Eduversity press

Made in the USA
Monee, IL
21 December 2024

75071901R00125